D1511775

A History of the LNER:
The Last Years, 1939–48

A History of the LNER: III. The Last Years, 1939-48

Michael R. Bonavia, M.A., Ph.D., F.C.I.T.

GUILD PUBLISHING
LONDON

This edition published 1985 by Book Club Associates by arrangement with
George Allen & Unwin

Picture research by Mike Esau

Set in 10 on 12 point Bembo by Nene Phototypesetters Ltd, Northampton
and printed and bound in Great Britain by
Biddles Ltd, Guildford and King's Lynn

Contents

Illustrations

Preface and Acknowledgments

The LNER had to struggle hard for most of its life. In its early years it was faced with problems of reorganisation coinciding with traffics declining owing to trade depression. In its middle years it achieved a notable degree of success in raising the level of rail travel to new standards of speed and comfort for this country, even though still denied an adequate rate of profit. In its last eight years, with which this volume is concerned, it coped strenuously with the handicaps imposed by war conditions and it planned boldly for a post-war return to a high quality of service – only to be faced with the battle that could not be won – the fight against nationalisation.

For this last instalment of the story of the LNER, I have drawn to some extent upon personal recollections of working for that great railway, but at least as much upon the recollections of friends and former colleagues, too numerous to list here, who have helped me in very many ways. I offer them my warmest thanks.

I am very grateful to Mr C. S. McLeod for the loan of the portrait of Robert Bell.

I must also express my thanks to Ian Allan Ltd for courteously permitting me to include in this book some passages from my articles on 'The Last Years of the LNER' published in *Railway World*.

M.R.B.

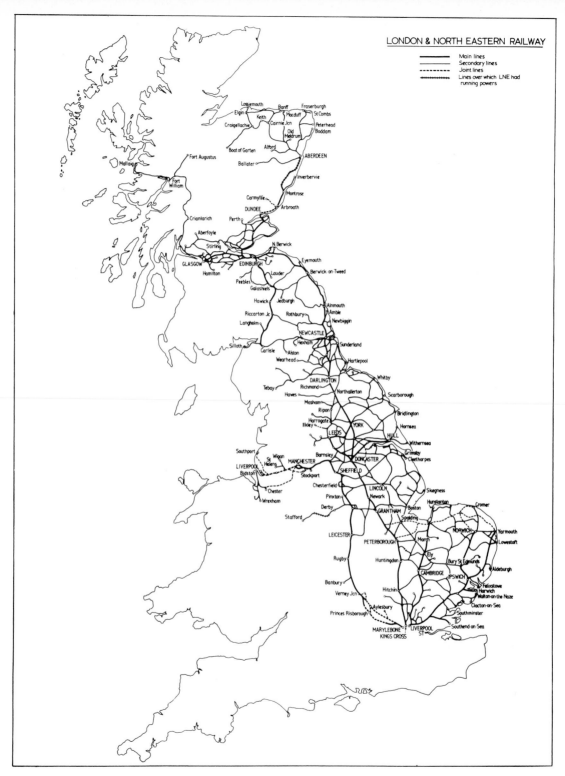

Frontispiece: London and North Eastern Railway route map.

I
The LNER Copes with War

On the morning of Friday 1 September 1939 New Barnet station on the Great Northern main line out of London was the scene of unusual activity. A poster had already warned passengers that after the morning peak hour only a skeleton service of suburban trains would operate. Instead, one long northbound train after another pulled, empty, into the station and was rapidly filled with hundreds of excited children who had emerged from a string of buses in the station courtyard. The buses had come in convoy from Enfield West station (since renamed Oakwood) on the Piccadilly Tube, a couple of miles away. Some of the trains into which the children piled were composed of suburban sets which had been released after the morning peak; others were scratch collections of main line vehicles.

Over at Enfield West, the Vice-Chairman of the London Passenger Transport Board, Frank Pick, (as his biographer, Christian Barman, has described) sat in his official car to watch the start of the operation. He had been the London Transport member of the Railway Executive Committee and was mainly responsible for the well-conceived evacuation plan which kept the children away from the congested London terminal stations and instead transferred them from Underground trains or buses to main line trains at suburban stations such as New Barnet, Stratford, Ealing Broadway, Watford and Wimbledon.

As the trains finished loading they pulled out for their destinations, the reception areas expected to be unlikely targets of enemy bombing. The work of King's Cross District at New Barnet and elsewhere was being matched by that of Stratford, where similar operations were in progress, sending children into the country areas of East Anglia. It was one of the most effective operations of the war and brought official thanks to the Railway Executive Committee and its Chairman, Sir Ralph Wedgwood. On his retirement from the Chief General Managership of the LNER in March 1939, Sir Ralph had been invited by the Minister of Transport to continue as chairman of the (then) purely advisory REC. He was subsequently asked to continue in office when war broke out and the REC became the essential link between the Government and the railways taken over 'for the duration'.

13

1. Children talking to the driver of an 'evacuation special', 24 September 1939.

All the railways had to face wartime problems such as operation under night-time black-out conditions; the release of staff for the Forces; bomb damage in air raids; shortage of supplies, especially of good quality locomotive coal; severely reduced maintenance standards, and the diversion of main workshops from railway to Government service. These have been fully recorded in several histories of the railways in wartime, so that it is only intended here to dwell on those features and incidents which were peculiar to the LNER.

If train operation was the most acute wartime problem facing the railways, it was gratifying to the LNER that throughout the six years of war, the chairmanship of the all-important Operating Committee of the REC was held by V. M. (later Sir Michael) Barrington-Ward. At the outbreak of war, 'B-W' was Superintendent (Southern Area), but later he was appointed Assistant General Manager (Operating) for the whole system. (The LNER's record in providing management talent in wartime recalled the precedent set by the North Eastern Railway in the war of 1914–18.)

In purely physical terms, the LNER entered the war with major problems. As a pre-dominantly freight line it was obviously going to carry a huge burden of Government traffic, which would have to be given priority over the regular passenger service. Moreover, serving the East Coast, it expected to suffer heavily from German air attacks. In the event, such attacks were not quite so concentrated on the 'drier side of Britain' – as LNER publicity called it – which suffered perhaps more from frequent intermittent raiding than from concentrated heavy blitzing such as that on Coventry, Manchester, Glasgow, Bristol, Plymouth or Liverpool. But Sheffield and Hull certainly experienced heavy bombing and the LNER 'caught it' particularly seriously in the London

area, especially the City, the Docks and the East End.

It was perhaps a handicap in some ways that Gresley's earlier locomotive policy had tended to concentrate upon express passenger designs, and building other types in relatively small batches – 'horses for courses', in fact. So the LNER was somewhat short of general-utility mixed-traffic locomotives such as the Stanier 'Black Fives' on the LMS or the GWR's Halls. But there was one versatile type that was to prove of great value to the railway, namely the V2 class of 2–6–2. These, supporting the Pacifics, performed splendid feats of haulage, handling long overloaded trains on (especially) the East Coast Main Line, throughout the war.

The LNER was to benefit considerably from the requisitioning of private owners' wagons which the Ministry of Transport effected in September 1939. These were brought into the railways' 'common user' pool and could thenceforth be used for any purpose for which they were suitable and available, instead of being returned when empty to their ownership centre.

New routeing instructions for freight were to eliminate the last vestiges of inter-company competition, under which a longer route was sometimes preferred in order to knock up the greatest mileage on the originating Company's metals. Another wartime innovation was the partial abandoning of engine 'diagramming', or planning in advance the duties of each loco-motive at a running shed. In wartime, shed-masters often had to assign the first suitable locomotive for duties as these arose, having regard to the huge increase in unscheduled services, controlled on a day-by-day or hour-by-hour basis, not by the printed timetable. Locomotives might turn up at sheds far from home and have to be worked back by any service that was available. This was responsible for some curiosities of operation, such as

2. Far from King's Cross and Liverpool Street: the LNER wartime H.Q.1.

Pacifics on heavy freights and goods engines on passenger trains.

The REC – like the Government – had expected intensive bombing to start immediately after the outbreak of war and had decided that only a skeleton passenger train service could be maintained – something like the Sunday services of pre-war days, though even slower, with overall average speeds not exceeding 45 mph and maximum running speeds everywhere limited to 60 mph. On 11 September 1939 time-sheets appeared at stations showing the new services. The 'Flying Scotsman', for instance, was replaced by a sort of *train omnibus* calling at all major stations between King's Cross and Edinburgh; it was terribly overcrowded. This service proved totally inadequate to meet the demand for travel, which continued at a high level.

Moreover, there was no bombing, and three weeks later the railways issued proper 'Emergency Time Tables' showing improved services. Even so the LNER booklet, dated 2 October 1939 – actually in *Bradshaw* format, and, rather ironically, marking the centenary of *Bradshaw* – showed passenger services which, compared with those of the previous August, were drastically slower, but even more drastically reduced in frequency, at any rate on the main lines, largely to provide more capacity for essential freight traffic. The splendid morning series of expresses leaving King's Cross in August was now reduced to a 10.00 to Edinburgh (a pale shadow of the 'Flying Scotsman', not arriving in the Northern capital until 7.30), a 10.30 for Leeds (5 hours 45 minutes) and a 12.30 to Newcastle (7 hours 5 minutes). Curiously the 10.00 am from King's Cross was booked to stand 15 minutes at Grantham; the

16

10.30 am to Leeds, 18 minutes at Peterborough. This, as Cecil J. Allen pointed out, recalled the old 20-minute interval at York for lunch before the days of restaurant cars. As the restaurant cars reappeared these long station stops were curtailed.

Savage cuts were made on the Great Central line, where there were only two daytime Manchester 'expresses' taking 6 hours 40 minutes (more or less) on the journey and one night train, with no 'fast' train leaving Marylebone between 10.00 am and 5 pm.

The Great Eastern Section did not seem to fare quite so badly, probably because, as its speeds had been somewhat lower, the 60 mph restriction did not make so much difference as, for instance, on the East Coast Main Line.

All LNER restaurant and buffet cars were withdrawn and only three sleeping car services were retained in this drastic re-timing.

But the absence of immediate enemy attacks during the eight months of the 1939–40 'phoney war' soon produced a demand for better rail services and new timetables for the LNER were issued on 4 December 1939. They considerably improved both frequency and – to some extent – journey times. A limited number of restaurant and buffet cars were restored and more sleeping cars provided.

Passenger travel remained at a high level throughout the war years for a number of reasons: petrol rationing stopped the use of cars for long journeys; Service travel was heavy at all times; many civilian visits were necessary owing to the evacuation of children and relatives; commuters had longer journeys or new journeys from having moved to 'safer' residential areas, and the strain of war made many people determined to obtain some sort of holiday, some change of surroundings, whatever happened. In view of these pressures official propaganda typified by the slogan 'Is

Your Journey Really Necessary?' had not much effect. The railways just had to cope as best they could.

The original Railway Executive Committee instruction for train working during air raids provided that after the warning had been given, passenger trains should stop at the next station, where passengers would be told of the raid and allowed to alight if they wished. The train would then proceed under 'caution' at a maximum speed of 15 mph. Freight trains would be stopped at the first signal-box and then be allowed to continue at not more than 10 mph.

This prevailed until warnings became much more frequent with the ending of the 'phoney war', when the consequent dislocation of train services began to have a serious effect on the war effort. So in November 1940 it was decided that passenger trains might run, after a warning, at 25 mph in daylight and 15 mph in darkness; and freight trains at 15 mph by day and night. Three months later the practice was changed again and in daylight all trains were allowed to run at normal speeds, engine drivers no longer being informed of 'Red' warnings. But during the night all trains were stopped and warned, and then allowed to continue at 30 mph.

Planning for operation under war conditions had acquired real momentum after the Munich crisis in the autumn of 1938. It was decided that, as London was expected to be the main centre of enemy bombing, railway offices must be provided with evacuation centres in safer areas. On the LNER the Secretary's office could be accommodated in the York office building and the Hotels Department of the Southern Area in the Felix Hotel at Felixstowe; the Area Rating Department was (surprisingly) to be found a temporary home in Peterborough station waiting room. But most moves were to be into accommodation just outside London. The Chief Accountant's staff was largely accommodated

Fox Photos

3. Guarding railway installations: a sentry on duty at Gas Works tunnel, King's Cross with V2 no. 4826 passing.

in rented houses at Hadley Wood. Similar premises were taken for the Goods Manager at South Woodford, and for the Advertising Manager at Stevenage.

The Chairman, Sir Ronald Matthews, decided that under war conditions he could not continue to live in his large country house, Aston Hall, about eight miles from Sheffield.

He moved into a tiny but very picturesque cottage at Letwell, near Worksop – retaining his London flat near to Marylebone station for weekday work – and rented Aston Hall to the LNER at a purely nominal rent of £100 pa. Aston Hall was assigned to the Sheffield District Goods Manager, the District Engineer and the Mineral Agent.

For security reasons it was decided to keep the

18

wartime location of some important departments as secret as possible, though obviously railway staff (and a good many other people) would be in the know. The Chief Mechanical Engineer's small headquarters staff from King's Cross was to move into his private house at Watton-at-Stone in Hertfordshire, henceforth referred to officially as H.Q.2.

H.Q.1, the LNER's central headquarters, was a large red-brick country house at Whitwell, near Knebworth in Hertfordshire. It was owned by Viscount Hampden and comprised, in the mansion, six reception rooms, fifteen bedrooms and seventeen servants' rooms, with seven acres of grounds.

Lord Hampden leased 'The Hoo', as the house was named, to the LNER for £1,100 a year for three years from 1939, and £500 a year thereafter for the remainder of a term of 21 years, the Company having an option to terminate the lease after three, seven or fourteen years.

Into 'The Hoo' moved the Chief General Manager and the Divisional General Manager, Southern Area with their staffs. The accommodation in the mansion was inadequate, so first of all the stable block was brought into use, and later a bungalow (for the Chief General Manager) and other temporary buildings were added. Even so, 'The Hoo' colony never reached quite the size of its LMS counterpart, 'The Grove', near Watford which assumed almost the appearance of a shanty town around the main house.

The planning of these moves owed much to Robert Bell's clear administrative mind. In June 1939 the CGM issued a circular to chief officers explaining that there would be two forms of wartime organisation, coded 'X' and 'Y'. Under Organisation X, 'Departments will, until further notice, carry out their functions from their existing locations and communication will be via the present telephone numbers . . . Under Organisation Y, departments located in London will be transferred to other centres. The general administration of the railway, together with the direction of the Southern Area departments will be carried out from one centre, to be designated H.Q.1.'

The circular explained that H.Q.1 would be manned night and day on a shift basis and that the institution of either Organisation would be signalled by means of a code telegram. In all, about 600 members of the staff would be moved, the new accommodation including in addition to the centres already mentioned, King's Lynn, Cambridge, Hunstanton, Peterborough and Retford.

Plan Y was duly notified and the changeover took place smoothly. The displaced staff experienced some initial discomfort but amenities were rapidly improved. At H.Q.1, in fact, a 'light weekly review' entitled *Ballyhoo Review* was produced as early as 26 September 1939, its editor being George Dow who had earlier that year succeeded E. G. Marsden as LNER Information Agent. Comprising 19 pages, it sold at the modest price of one (old) penny (less than 1/2p). It helped to raise morale among the evacuees.

2
The Effects of the War

Each of the main phases of the war had its effect upon the railway. The 'phoney war' was followed by the Dunkirk evacuation; then came night bombing and the intensification of rearmament; the build-up to D-day and the flying bomb and rocket attacks. All these enforced new railway operating practices and made new demands upon resources. One handicap persisted throughout 5½ years of war – that of the black-out. Marshalling yards suffered from lack of lighting at night; engine crews had to endure tarpaulin sheeting stretched from the cab roof to the tender to obscure the glare from the firehole door; station platforms were dimly lit, and station names almost impossible to discern. Drivers had to approach stations very cautiously in order to bring trains to a stand at a platform. Protective hoods were extended over colour-light signals and in many cases their light intensity had to be drastically reduced following air raid warnings.

At the LNER docks, the black-out at Grimsby and Immingham was responsible for 150 people falling into the water, 41 of whom drowned.

Black-out regulations were slightly eased after a time to enable the railway to work under fewer handicaps. Three main lighting categories were established, the most restrictive being maintained in coastal areas. Master switches were installed at some centres in order that all railway lighting could be instantly turned down on receipt of a 'Red' or 'Purple' air raid warning: at other times a barely adequate lighting standard could be maintained.

Early in the war, but fortunately before the heavy air attacks had begun, the LNER experienced some of the worst winter weather recorded. On 29 January 1940 a snowstorm blocked the Manchester–Sheffield main line for several days; the locomotive of a ballast train was buried up to its chimney. The West Highland line was also blocked and only the efforts of 200 railway staff and 200 soldiers sufficed to free a snow-plough which, with two propelling engines, was locked in a snowdrift; train services were suspended for a fortnight.

Operation Dynamo – the evacuation through Dunkirk – affected the LNER rather less than the other three main line railways though, as Norman Crump records in *By Rail to Victory*,

A fair proportion of the Dunkirk specials to the north came up via Oxford and Banbury where they passed on to the old Great Central line which carried them on via Woodford and

---

4. A rail link of great wartime importance: the Forth Bridge.

Leicester. At Leicester, ablution benches were set up on the platform, to give the men fresh from Dunkirk a chance to get a wash. During June 1940, 242 special trains, including a number of the Dunkirk trains, passed through Leicester. Others went round the west of London and passed on to the Great Central section at Neasden.

Diversion in 1940 from coastwise shipping to rail of coal traffic from the North-East to London and the South involved the operation of convoy coal trains – foreshadowing the block trains of the post-war era – largely passing over the East Coast Main Line. Finding paths for these trains, together with specials carrying urgent Government traffic, caused the passenger services between King's Cross, Newcastle and Scotland to be reduced once more, with restaurant cars again being taken off and the number of sleeping cars curtailed. Restaurant cars were gradually restored but again reduced in May 1942; finally all restaurant cars were taken off at Easter 1944 on Ministry of War Transport instructions.

The length of trains had to be increased to compensate for the reduction in frequency, 20-coach trains being quite common. This, in addition to putting a strain on engine power, meant frequent drawing up at platforms to enable every passenger to alight. At King's Cross there were special difficulties, as such very long trains could foul the adjacent platform roads and prevent train movements into or out of them. At times this was solved by restricting trains of empty coaches, brought into a departure platform, to the length of the platform; the locomotive would back on with additional coaches at the head of the train just before departure time. Arriving trains were divided and stationed in two platforms.

Heaving these heavy trains out through Gas Works Tunnel could be a problem, even for a Pacific or a V2; one wondered why the carriage pilot that had brought in the empty coaches could not bank the departing train at least as far as the platform end. King's Cross practice forbade this, allegedly because many years ago there had been a derailment in Gas Works Tunnel from over-energetic banking.

Probably the record passenger train length on the LNER was achieved on 31 March 1940 when the 10.45 am from Newcastle was strengthened at Peterborough to make up no less than 26 coaches, weighing about 762 tons tare or 850 tons gross. V2 no. 4800 worked the train into King's Cross in 103 minutes – only nine minutes over the scheduled time.

The experience of evacuating children in 1939 was repeated on a smaller scale in May 1940 when invasion was believed to be imminent. Children had originally been taken to some East Anglian centres such as Clacton, Felixstowe, Walton and Woodbridge; now they had to be moved to South Wales, remote from the likely invasion areas. Another mass evacuation exercise was carried out during the period of flying bombs in 1944; by this time the operating procedures had become virtually standardised.

The total extent of bomb damage on the LNER is difficult to summarise. Of course, the first big raids on London, which concentrated upon the docks and the East End, hit the railway very seriously. One day saw the Liverpool Street–Cambridge main line blocked at London Fields whilst there were bombs at Shadwell, Fenchurch Street, Gas Factory Junction, Custom House, Canning Town and Bethnal Green. Liverpool Street station was hit several times, with bombs on platforms nos 1, 4 and 18. A delayed-action bomb in the engine sidings at the country end of no. 10 platform later exploded, killing two railwaymen who were carrying on with their work after four wagons

J. G. Dewing

5. An ex-Metropolitan Railway H2 4–4–4T no. 6415 now in LNER stock hauls a London Transport Aylesbury train past a 'gas spray detector board' near Chorley Wood in June 1940.

loaded with ballast had been placed in position to act as a screen. The DGM's headquarters offices at Liverpool Street were badly damaged on 10–11 May 1941, underlining the wisdom of the move to H.Q.1.

King's Cross suffered in the same night from two 1,000-lb bombs chained together which fell on the General Offices alongside the (then) no. 10 platform (present no. 8) bringing down a large section of the main roof span on top of a newspaper train standing at no. 10. Marylebone passenger station had no direct hit, but the Goods station – the splendidly spacious one constructed by the GCR in the hope of extensive freight business from the London Extension – was largely burnt out by incendiary bombs on the night of 16 April 1941. On two occasions Marylebone passenger station was put out of action by bombs on the tunnels in the St John's Wood area; part of the shallow tunnel at Carlton

6. Temporary roll-on, roll-off rail overbridge for wartime use at Northallerton.

Hill had to be opened up permanently as a cutting.

The whole of King's Cross District suffered from bombs at Holloway, Finsbury Park, Barnet and other places. Trains were kept moving only by the efforts of a resolute staff (several of whom were killed on duty) led by W. E. Green, the District Superintendent who took over at a critical time and earned an MBE for his efforts.

The bombing elsewhere paralleled the experiences of London, though usually not on so prolonged a scale. Hull was heavily bombed on 7 May 1941 and the docks were, of course, a special target on many other occasions. Paragon station survived amid surroundings of com-pletely destroyed buildings, but the effect upon the railway operation of over 100 raids up to February 1944 speaks for itself. Newcastle suffered much less, and York had only one serious raid in which the station was hit whilst the 'Night Scotsman' was standing at no. 9 platform. Part of the train was set on fire, the passengers having been evacuated on receipt of the 'Red' alert; the coaches on either side of those on fire were uncoupled and drawn clear, forwards and back respectively, whilst the raid continued. Adding insult to injury, A4 Pacific no. 4466, 'Sir Ralph Wedgwood', was destroyed in the station by a bomb.

Trains were sometimes attacked by enemy aircraft, the most spectacular case being that of the 'Flying Scotsman' which on 11 November

7. A4 no. 10, 'Dominion of Canada', still carrying the presentation bell, but grimy in war service.

1941 was a victim at Marshall Meadows just north of Berwick (the boundary point between the North Eastern and Scottish Areas). Two planes dropped bombs which missed the train and then machine-gunned it from end to end, fortunately without casualties other than a bullet wound in the fireman's arm.

After the relative lull in bombing during 1942 and 1943, the 'V' bombs resumed the offensive in a new form in June 1944 and the concentration of these weapons on the London area presented the LNER with fresh problems. 'Doodle-bugs' hit Finsbury Park, Neasden yard, Marylebone Passenger signal-box, Stratford and other spots; and the very short interval (two minutes at most) between a 'Red' alert and the first explosions, made it very difficult to devise any adequate warning system for trainmen. Improvised signs such as a board with an

25

T. G. Hepburn. Rail Archive Stephenson

8. 'How are the mighty fallen!' A4 no. 22, 'Mallard', proud holder of the world's speed record with steam traction, grimy and leaking steam at Grantham shed in 1947.

arrow pointing skywards were eventually hung out of the window by signalmen to warn drivers to proceed at caution during flying bomb attacks. No warning system at all, however, could be developed to cope with the V2 rockets which from September 1944 to March 1945 fell intermittently on London and hit various points on the LNER including Palmers Green, Stratford, Lea Bridge Road, Channelsea, Angel Road and Wood Green. The LNER publicity reported after the end of the war that one out of every seven rockets which fell in this country had either hit the LNER or interfered with it.

In addition to obvious physical damage, the railway suffered in more subtle ways. Locomotive maintenance at running sheds could not approach peacetime standards, and cleaning, except for the motion, came to an end 'for the duration'. New construction was limited to mixed-traffic and freight types, and main workshops were partly diverted to the production of war materials.

Carriage and wagon shops also saw some of their capacity taken up in this way, with consequent effects upon the condition of rolling stock in traffic. Doncaster and York shops combined to make glider parts, and Cowlairs and Gorton aeroplane and tank parts. Doncaster assembled gun mountings manufactured there and also at Darlington, Stratford and Cowlairs. Shildon Wagon Works made gun carriage forgings, as did Gorton. The LNER adapted two shops at Dukinfield near Manchester and embarked upon shell production, a task personally supervised by Gresley. Shildon also went into the manufacture of ball bearings when supplies of these from overseas were cut off.

Staff numbers fell at the outset of the war owing to the men enrolled in the Territorial Army being called up. The LNER provided, within the Army Supplementary Reserve (Royal Engineers), an Operating Company, a Docks Group and two Railway Construction Companies. These units, as Robert Bell has written 'were composed of picked railwaymen, including many young and energetic officers.'

Railwaymen were not subject to complete reservation from the call-up. Different reservation ages were fixed for different grades. Of course, numbers of railwaymen volunteered for patriotic reasons. Overall, the LNER contributed its full quota to the total for the four main line railways of 98,603 men and 3,129 women released to H.M. Forces throughout the war period. Somehow the staffing gap had to be filled. The problem was not serious in the early months of the war, as new entrants could be found to replace those leaving, but the build-up of recruitment and also the attraction of munitions work, paid at higher rates than railway work, caused a serious drift away in 1940–1, which was only checked by the Essential Work Order, applied to the railways in October 1941, stopping railway staff from changing their jobs without permission. Even so, the manpower crisis worsened with the heavy workload imposed on the railways and from May 1942 no call-up from the operating grades to the Forces was effected unless the Company agreed to it.

The peak traffics before D-day in 1944 created a crisis due to a shortage of footplate staff, mainly firemen. Staff were recruited outside the established line of promotion and some men were lent from the Forces to tide the railway over the critical period. Of course, women were also being recruited to fill many posts normally filled by men – well over 15,000 on the LNER being so employed.

Although much of the work of the women, for instance in signal-boxes, was not obvious to the travelling public, some exceptions occurred. For instance, regular travellers on the Great Sheffield to Marylebone services became aware of two women travelling Train Attendants, known to 'regulars' as Mary and Alice. These ladies had been promoted from carriage cleaning duties and were equipped with thick dark blue serge uniforms that hardly matched the smartness expected of air hostesses. They were, however, popular with passengers for their unfailing cheerfulness and especially (in the absence of restaurant car services) for the coffee which they dispensed from thermos flasks to a sort of club that forgathered in the brake van after receiving a secret signal from Mary or Alice as they passed down the corridor and glanced into the compartments occupied by regular passengers favoured in this way. The coffee club was *not* on a cash basis; but naturally the popular hostesses received small gifts in the shape of some chocolate or cigarettes from time to time – very acceptable when such little luxuries were rationed.

3
The Sinews of War

It was obviously unreasonable to expect the railways to carry the huge extra burden of war traffic without some strengthening of resources. But initially it took strenuous efforts on the part of the Railway Executive Committee of General Managers to persuade the Government – meaning senior civil servants and Ministers – of this unpalatable fact. The LNER's financial problems in peacetime had not permitted it to invest in building up spare capacity from its own resources, and the special works programmes financed under the Development (Loan Guarantees and Grants) Act 1929 and the Railways Agreement Act 1935, had gone only a very small part of the way to provide some of the new facilities needed in wartime.

An immediate need was to forestall one possible effect of heavy enemy bombing on railways in the London area by providing more routes for North/South traffic in addition to the cross-London routes used in peacetime – the Metropolitan 'Widened Lines', the East London Railway, the West London line, and the North and South West Junction Railway. The Government agreed to finance the rapid construction of new connections, several of which concerned the LNER. A single-line spur was built at Harringay to link the GN main line with the Tottenham and Hampstead Joint Line, and a link at Gospel Oak between the T&H and the LMS North London Line, enabling the LNER to send traffic to the Southern Railway by either the West London or the North & South West Junction, instead of the East London or the 'Widened Lines'.

A link between the GN and GE lines was inserted at Bounds Green, so that traffic from the North via the Hertford loop could pass on to the GE if the GN main line was blocked anywhere south of Langley Junction, near Stevenage.

Away from London, a main North/South route was via Oxford and Reading to the Southern, either via Basingstoke or via Staines. But its capacity was limited and possible diversions were arranged by a connection at Sandy on the GN main line which enabled the LMS Cambridge to Bletchley route to be used, together with another connection at Calvert between the Oxford–Bletchley line and the GC main line.

Between Northallerton and York the LNER suffered from bottlenecks at Thirsk, Sessay, Raskelf and Skelton Bridge near York, even though most of the route had been four-tracked. It was heavily occupied in peacetime by East Coast passenger trains, through freight between England and Scotland, and the very heavy in-

M. N. Clay. Rail Archive Stephenson

9. Plugging away in wartime: ex-NER J24 no. 1892 piloting J27 no. 2384 with a train of petrol tanks in the North East in 1942.

dustrial traffic of the Tyne, Tees and Wear areas passing both south and west. The convoy coal trains aggravated an already serious problem and widenings were put in hand between Pilmoor and Thirsk. Pilmoor, Thirsk and Sessay stations were partly rebuilt, and a new bridge over the River Ouse was built for the widening near York. An avoiding line at Northallerton was also built as a precaution against this key junction being put out of action, its importance stemming from the fact that the East Coast Main Line was here joined by the line from Leeds at the South end, and at the North end by the Tees-side line, as well as the single-line Hawes branch connecting with the Midland main line in the heart of the Pennines. The levels and gradients imposed a five-foot clearance between the new avoiding line and the Hawes branch. An unusual solution was found to this difficulty in the shape of a temporary overbridge on the Hawes branch which ran on rollers and could be moved out of the way quickly should it be necessary to bring the avoiding line into use. (The Hawes branch, in that case, could still be reached by a reversal and the use of a triangular spur.)

Another unusual development was the new line constructed to serve a group of munitions factories – dispersed to minimise the consequence of any explosion – at Thorp Arch on the line from Church Fenton to Harrogate. It employed 18,000 workers on a three-shift basis

10. Ack-ack guns being built in an LNER workshop.

and the LNER was asked to provide rail services for the workers from Leeds and elsewhere coming to the new 'green fields' site or leaving it, three times in every 24 hours. A roughly circular single line of railway, 6½ miles long, was constructed serving the main factories at four stations, in addition to the main one at Thorp Arch. Trains ran in one direction only, much as they had done over the loop to the Wembley Exhibition station in 1924, calling at each station. The line's capacity was substantial as it was equipped with automatic colour-light signalling.

Less extensive but still substantial facilities for munition workers were provided at Aycliffe, a few miles North of Darlington, where twenty trains a day served the factories.

Considerable railway works were required at Faslane, 'Emergency Port No. 1' on the Gareloch, so extensively used for the ships taking part in the landings in North Africa in the autumn of 1942. The rail connection was from the West Highland line of the Scottish Area, on a steeply falling gradient which presented an operating problem.

The total outlay on Ministry of War Transport works for the LNER amounted to £3,571,000. Rather optimistically, Robert Bell wrote in 1945 that these works – running lines, sidings, signalling and other installations – 'represent a valuable addition to our transport equipment, provided that the quantity of post-war commercial traffic is sufficient to keep them in constant use.' Sadly, this condition has not been met in BR days.

11. On loan to the LNER: a Ministry of Supply 2–10–0 designed for service overseas.

Locomotive construction during the war was, on Ministry instructions, confined to freight or mixed-traffic types. An initial standard design was chosen, the Stanier 8F 2–8–0 freight loco-motive, of which the LNER built over 100 at Doncaster and Darlington. In 1942, in order to economise as much as possible in the use of scarce materials, the 2–8–0 Austerity version – a modification of the Stanier design – was developed for the Ministry of Supply by the North British Locomotive Company, with the LMS Chief Draughtsman acting as adviser. These engines were intended for eventual service overseas and were built in large numbers by both the North British Locomotive Com-pany and the Vulcan Foundry. The LNER benefited by being lent over 500 until they were required for shipment, as well as a small number of 2–10–0 freight engines ordered by the Ministry for difficult routes overseas, especially in Persia (Iran). The LNER was also allotted

168 American 2–8–0 locomotives designed for use on the Continent, pending the invasion – welcome assistance at a time when traffic was building up to a peak.

Against this the LNER in 1939 had had to lend the GWR 40 0–6–0 goods locomotives as a partial recompense for GWR engines transferred to the War Office for overseas use. The LNER also furnished 35 tank engines for Government work, 16 of which were allocated to work armoured trains near the coast. Again, no less than 92 2–8–0 class 04 engines (ex-GCR Robinson design) were sent to Persia (Iran), to work on trains taking war supplies to Russia.

Passenger carriage construction of a normal character came to a halt during the war, the carriage shops at York, Cowlairs and Dukin-field being engaged on war work. But 290 vehicles for ambulance trains were built by the LNER, as well as several special trains for VIPs. General Eisenhower wrote a warm letter of thanks to Sir Ronald Matthews for the armour-plated LNER vehicle which was constructed for

Fox Photos

14. The great snowfall in the first winter of the war traps a train on the Manchester–Sheffield line on 7 February 1940. Even the snow-plough is stuck.

12. *(upper left)* An Austerity 2–8–0 on the GW and GC Joint Line near Beaconsfield with a freight train.

13. *(left)* V2 no. 3655 heading south from Retford with a train of Churchill tanks in September 1943.

his personal use, code-named 'Bayonet'. The LNER also provided the special train, code-named 'Rapier', for the use of the C-in-C Home Forces.

Wagons, as distinct from passenger carriages, were deemed essential to the war effort and so continued to be built, including 'Warflats' and 'Warwells' for conveyance of tanks. The Ministry of War Transport sponsored a new all-steel 16-ton coal wagon of which very large numbers were built; they were an improvement on the 10-ton or 12-ton wooden wagons of which so many thousands were still in use, but scarcely as effective as the ex-NER 20-ton hoppers used in conjunction with bottom discharge at shipping staithes or coal 'cells' at stations.

It eventually fell, not to the LNER, but to the nationalised British Railways, to decide which of the new assets provided to meet war requirements and paid for by the Government, would have continuing usefulness in peacetime and should be taken over at a price to be negotiated. Not many of them met this criterion.

4
'Incidents' and Accidents

The all-embracing but vague term 'incident' was used during the war, for censorship reasons, to describe a wide range of unpleasant happenings. But whereas railway accidents too often have been due to human failure, to some error of judgment or slackness which might carry a disciplinary penalty, wartime 'incidents' often evoked courage and initiative greatly deserving of recognition. It was with this in mind that the Chairman of the LNER proposed at a meeting of the wartime Emergency Board held at York on 28 November 1940 a resolution 'that the Company institute a silver medal for award to members of the Company's staff for acts of bravery in connection with the War.' The Board resolved accordingly and a medal was designed by Gilbert Bayes, PRBS, bearing the LNER crest on one side and on the reverse the words 'For Courage and Resource'.

The medal was awarded a total of twenty-two times between January 1942 and November 1947. It has been suggested that the time elapsed between approval of the idea of a medal and the first award was due to some official objections to a railway company exercising what is normally considered to be the Royal prerogative. However, the LNER files have not revealed any correspondence confirming this suggestion. It may be added that eighty-eight members of the LNER staff serving with the Forces received decorations between September 1939 and April 1944.

Of the twenty-two awards of the LNER medal, two, associated with the same incident, stand out. The story of the Soham explosion will bear retelling.

Driver B. Gimbert and Fireman J. Nightall booked on at 10.10 pm on 1 June 1944, taking no. WD77337 (an Austerity 2–8–0) to work the 11.40 pm booked from Whitemoor to Goodmayes yard on the GE Colchester main line. The train was, however, diverted to White Colne, on the Colne Valley line, which was to be reached by a circuitous cross-country route via Ely (Dock Junction), the single-line section to Fordham, then (bypassing Newmarket on the spur line) via Bury St Edmunds, Ipswich and Marks Tey to destination – a real Cook's tour of East Anglia, and one illustrative of the new routes brought into use in wartime.

The train load was 51 wagons of bombs and the wagon next to the engine contained 40 500-lb bombs. All went normally until the single-line section after Ely had been entered when, passing the Soham distant signal, at between 15 and 20 mph, Driver Gimbert saw that the first wagon behind the tender was on

15. The LNER Medal.

forward, Gimbert's intention being to get it clear of the built-up area, leave it standing uncoupled, and go forward with the engine to Fordham, the next station. As he passed the signal-box he called to the signalman, to ascertain that there was no 'train on line', coming from Fordham; but at that instant the wagon exploded, making a crater 66 feet in diameter and 15 feet deep. It entirely demolished the station and the stationmaster's house. Damage of one sort or another was done to some 700 houses in Soham: but if the whole train had exploded, the town must have been virtually flattened.

Fireman Nightall was killed and Driver Gimbert seriously injured. At a ceremony in the Board Room at Marylebone station, Sir Ronald Matthews presented the LNER Medal to Gimbert and to Nightall's widow. This supplemented the highest civilian decoration for gallantry, the George Cross which was also awarded to Gimbert and, posthumously, to Nightall. The grateful inhabitants of Soham placed a memorial tablet in the temporary station that replaced the one destroyed in the explosion. And nearly 40 years later a class 47 diesel locomotive bears the name-plate 'Benjamin Gimbert, G.C.'.

There were a score of other well-deserved presentations at Marylebone; but the Soham 'incident' is remembered as outstanding for the qualities displayed by two railwaymen who, in the appalling circumstances in which they found themselves, might well have jumped from the footplate and run for cover, instead of coolly carrying out the correct procedures with death staring them in the face.

Accident reporting was often curtailed for security reasons during the war. However, it was revealed in 1942 that an unusual accident occurred on the GC Section, on 11 February, close to Beighton station. A heavy steel plate in

fire. He sounded the whistle to warn the guard and then – carefully, in view of the train's load – stopped by the station end of the goods shed. Fireman Nightall descended and uncoupled the first wagon from the rest of the train, then rejoined the engine, which drew slowly

16. Soham station before the explosion.

British Rail

course of transit from the Frodingham steel-works was displaced when the wagon carrying it was shunted, and it became embedded in the side of a passing troop train, causing the death of 14 soldiers and serious injury to 35 others.

A much less serious accident happened at King's Cross on 4 February 1945, when the 6 pm King's Cross to Leeds became stalled in Gas Works Tunnel and actually began to move backwards. Emerging from the tunnel, the coaches collided with the front of the 7 pm 'Aberdonian', standing in no. 10 platform. The most serious aspect of this collision at low speed was that the moving coaches rose in the air and demolished the gantry with signals, platform indicators and shunting discs. It took a fortnight before a new signal gantry could be positioned and meanwhile suburban services were terminated at Finsbury Park and main line train

movements from the west side of the station were controlled by hand signals.

After the war ended and before the LNER was 'vested' in the British Transport Commission's Railway Executive, there were two accidents, both in 1946; and also another in 1947 which had much more serious consequences. In 1946 it was curious that *two* derailments took place within a short space of time near Hatfield on the GN main line – that line whose permanent way had been generally considered to be the pride of the LNER, but which had been punished by the heavy wartime traffics.

On 15 July the 7.5 pm from King's Cross to Aberdeen, hauled by a V2 2–6–2, became derailed on the curve at Hatfield but, miraculously, no one was killed. A feature of this accident was that two schoolboy train spotters were sitting on a fence opposite the site of the

36

17. Soham after the explosion on 2 June 1944.

derailment and were able to describe accurately the exact sequence of events. 'The tender was going one way and the boiler another. The wobble was sideways "like a snake". After the engine had passed . . . the front wheels came off first and the two back wheels became dislodged later.'

Four months later, on 10 November, at Marshmoor, between Brookmans Park and Hatfield, the 4.45 pm from Newcastle to King's Cross, also hauled by a V2, was derailed but, fortunately, the coaches remained upright and there were no serious casualties.

Whilst it was clear in each case that the track

18. Driver Gimbert's engine after the explosion.

Keystone Press Agency

alignment was defective and was the prime cause of the derailment, the Inspecting Officer considered that a contributory cause was the design of the swing link control of the engine's leading pony truck, which reacted adversely to small defects in track cross-levels and alignment.

Modifications to the V2 class were put in hand, and it was decided that as new Pacifics entered service from the post-war building programmes, the V2 class should be relegated from express passenger work to the mixed-traffic work for which they had originally been designed.

19. Liverpool Street station, September 1940.

The last important accident during the lifetime of the LNER, unhappily a very serious one, occurred the following year, on 27 October 1947, at Goswick, between Berwick and Newcastle on the East Coast Main Line. This was caused by the combination of a driver ignoring a diversion notice, and by a signalman's error of judgment.

On the day in question, a Sunday, the engineers had possession of the up main line at Goswick; trains were being diverted to the up independent line, with a severe speed restriction over the turnout. The driver of the 11.15 am Edinburgh–King's Cross train booked on at Haymarket shed but failed to read the diversion notice; he also took 'an unauthorised person' on the footplate with him, which may have caused some loss of concentration on signals.

At Goswick, the signalman's procedure was to leave his up distant at 'caution', and when an approaching train had slowed down sufficiently, to clear the home signal, draw the train forward slowly to the starter and then display a green flag (at that date still the colour for a 'caution' given by flag signal) whilst lowering the starter controlling the turnout to the up independent line.

Approaching Goswick the driver failed to read the distant, owing (he said later) to its being obscured by steam from the engine. The signalman also saw steam coming from the safety valves and assumed that this was due to the regulator having been closed and brakes applied. He thereupon mistakenly lowered his home signal.

The driver was not in fact braking and, seeing the home signal come off, assumed that he had a clear run on the main line. As the train approached the turnout the signalman realised that its speed was excessive. He threw back the home signal to danger and pulled the detonator placer lever.

But the warning came too late; the locomotive and eight coaches were derailed and fell away from the track into a ditch. Twenty-seven passengers were killed and 59 persons, including the driver and fireman, seriously injured.

This accident had parallels with others where Sunday diversions were involved and where a driver had ignored or forgotten a diversion notice until too late. The Inspecting Officer in his report pointed out that some form of audible warning at the distant signal would probably have been effective in preventing this type of accident; but this device was not to be extended to the East Coast Main Line until well into British Railways days.

5
The Gratitude of Government

As might be expected from its title, this is a very short chapter! Certainly, at the end of the war the Chairman of the Railway Companies Association received a letter of official thanks for the splendid work the railways had performed in the past six years. But more tangible expressions of gratitude were totally absent. In fact, although it has only recently come to light through the opening to researchers of Government files in the Public Record Office, senior civil servants during the war had already decided in their own minds that, as one of them put it in an official minute, 'the railways are obviously ripe for nationalisation.'

The LNER had been placed under Government control from 1 September 1939 by means of the Emergency (Railway Control) Order 1939, issued under the Emergency Powers (Defence) Act, and forthwith the Railway Executive Committee became agents of the Minister. But how were the railways to be paid for this takeover of their undertakings? There had been preliminary talks about this during 1937, when the railways had argued that they should in wartime be guaranteed their 'standard revenue' under the 1921 Railways Act, although this had never been earned in peacetime, because under war conditions they would obviously be carrying greatly increased traffics.

The Government rejected this argument but agreed instead that its guarantee of net revenue should be based on the actual earnings of the Companies, averaged over the three years immediately before the war. This was later modified to the average of 1935, 1936 and 1937 because of the 'hiccup' in 1938, after which revenue had recovered in 1939.

In February 1940 Parliament was told of the terms agreed with the railways, which involved the pooling of expenditure and receipts of the four main line railways and the London Passenger Transport Board. Of the net receipts in the pool, the LNER was to receive 23 per cent, subject to a guaranteed minimum of £9.2 millions. Any excess of net receipts would be shared on a sliding scale between the railways and the Government; but the railways would never get more than their 'standard revenue' under the 1921 Act.

But in September 1941 the Minister of War Transport told Parliament, in a White Paper,

20. The effect of the raid at Middlesbrough.

that revised arrangements had now been agreed. This was technically correct, although the Railway Companies had had considerable misgivings about the new 'agreement'. So far as the LNER was concerned, instead of the sliding scale for revenue to be shared with the Government, a new fixed annual rent of £10.1 million was imposed – a small increase on the 'floor' of £9.2 million but well below the 'ceiling' of £15.2 million under the original 1940 arrangement. Provision was made for an Arrears of Maintenance Trust Fund, which, the White Paper stated, at the end of the control period (which 'will be continued for a minimum period of one year after the cessation of hostilities') was to be available to overtake the arrears of maintenance imposed on the Companies by war conditions.

The LNER Stockholders Association raised the question of the Control Agreement at the LNER Annual General Meeting in 1944, and urged the Board to represent to the Government that the 1941 Agreement was unfair to the Company. Similar resolutions, sponsored by the British Railway Stockholders' Union, were passed at the meetings of the three other Companies. The argument was that the volume of work performed by the railways, much of it on Government account, had fully justified the net revenue being raised to the level of 'standard revenue'.

The Chairmen of the four Railway Companies met the Minister of War Transport on 20 April 1944 and, as Robert Bell has recorded, they 'pointed out that the extension of the war area in December 1941 had thrown a far greater burden on the railways than was contemplated when the agreement was negotiated. The great expansion of traffic had caused a more intensive use of the capital assets employed, and it was unfair that the basic figure of maintenance should be limited to the levels of the years 1935–6–7.'

21. York after the 'Baedeker' raid.

The Government rejected the argument on net revenue, but agreed to look again at 'abnormal wear and tear'. This proved to be of little practical value to the LNER, since at the end of the war the control period was extended right up to the date of nationalisation, 1 January 1948.

After the end of hostilities in 1945, the LNER entered a period of great uncertainty, a new Labour Government having promised nationalisation, and shortages of essential materials making it impossible to overtake the arrears of maintenance in physical terms. The Board, therefore, had its hands tied; share-holders received their fixed net revenue under the 1941 agreement, but the opportunity was denied the railway to participate in the profits from the continuing post-war traffic levels which were boosted by petrol rationing and limits upon motor vehicle construction. They were also unable to raise charges so as properly to reflect increased costs. 'RB' pointed out that, for the main line railways together, the fixed rentals had only amounted to about one-half of the actual net earnings of the railways between 1941 and 1944 inclusive.

Moreover, in measuring the gross receipts, it must not be forgotten that Government traffic, representing a very large proportion of the total, was carried at rates below the standard, on a basis originally negotiated in 1941, and later at flat rates which represented a considerable saving on the notional 'commercial' charges. If a normal railway/consignor relationship had existed, the railways' gross receipts would have been much higher. As it was, the Government saved a great deal of money at the expense of the railway stockholders, whose reward was to see their holdings confiscated in January 1948, on terms which, Sir Ronald Matthews picturesquely declared, 'would bring a blush of shame to the leathery cheek of a Barbary pirate.'

43

6
Planning for the Post-War World

When the war ended the railways had already undertaken a considerable amount of planning for their role in the post-war world. The Railway Companies Association (in effect the four Chairmen) had set up a Post-War Planning Commission under Colonel Sir Eric Gore-Browne, then Deputy Chairman of the Southern Railway, which had prepared a set of very far-reaching proposals. These involved the virtual unification of the railways. One may guess that this would have been acceptable to William Whitelaw with his rather advanced views on nationalisation, by no means shared by his brother chairmen. But Sir Ronald Matthews, who had strong Conservative Party connections, took a very cautious view of the Gore-Browne report, as did the General Managers, to whom it was remitted for comment regarding its practical implications. However, the LNER went along with the more modest proposals eventually agreed within the Railway Companies Association for an extension of co-operation, especially with the LMS, including a possible exchange of 'penetrating lines'. It was hoped also to co-operate with road haulage interests, partly through extended investment in road under-takings, partly through agreement on rate policy on the lines of the pre-war 'Square Deal'. Many technical improvements, including ideas imported from America – baggage registration and luggage lockers at stations among them – were envisaged.

The LNER concentrated upon the physical improvements to the system that it wanted to effect as soon as Government restrictions, and the release of the money in the Arrears of Maintenance Trust Fund, would permit. A Committee of officers was set up to devise a programme of works; it was composed of the three Assistant Divisional General Managers, under the chairmanship of James Ness, then Assistant (Works and General) to the Chief General Manager. The works were grouped into a First Priority and a Second Priority List, the estimated cost totalling about £25 million. The split was:

	£m.
All-line departments	2½
Southern Area	10
North Eastern Area	6
Scottish Area	4
Acquisition of MWT Works	2½
	25

22. South Lynn, April 1947; an ex-M&GN shunter with 'N.E.' lettering but with an unmistakable ex-MR Salter spring-balance and 'coffee-pot' safety valves of a bygone age.

H. C. Casserley

23. Long Melford Junction: one of the delightful East Anglian rural backwaters which 'progress' was to sweep away after nationalisation.   *W. Philip Conolly*

T. G. Hepburn. Rail Archive Stephenson

24. V2 no. 832 leaves Scarborough with an up express in June 1947.

Among major schemes were the reconstruction of King's Cross frontage and concourse; Peterborough station rebuilding; the Greenwood–Potters Bar widening; various new marshalling yards and freight terminals; running line facilities and colour-light signalling at many places.

The substantial volume describing these schemes was nicknamed the 'Rainbow Book' because the various sections were printed on differently coloured paper. I produced a shortened version, fully illustrated, as a publicity exercise. It was called *Forward: the LNER Development Programme* and it incorporated line

25. The 'Newton' coach.

diagrams with all the principal improvements envisaged described in 'boxes' on either side.

The ambitious nature of the LNER's planning contrasted sharply with the actual standstill on new works imposed by the Government's perpetuation of the control period and by the uncertainty created through the threat of nationalisation. It was ironical that, when the Beveridge proposals for the Welfare State were being so energetically implemented, the physical framework of the economy in the shape of transport infrastructure should be given such a low priority, especially when on the Continent the German, French, Italian and Dutch railways were being strongly supported by their Governments in fully rehabilitating and modernising their systems.

Paper planning in official circles, far removed from authorising any physical works, continued at a high and quite unrealistic level. The LNER had to take note of the proposals in the 1943 County of London Plan (the Forshaw-Abercrombie Report) containing some vague but sweeping suggestions affecting the LNER, the principal being, 'At Liverpool Street the present site might be utilised for an underground station for suburban lines, with a new main line station on the site of the present Bishopsgate Goods station, and connected by a low level loop with a new station replacing the present Fenchurch Street station.'

Later, in 1944, Professor Abercrombie, this time on his own, published the Greater London Plan. The stated object was to discourage

26. Ex-GNR D3 4—4—0 no. 2000, with the LNER crest on the tender, as used for hauling the Directors' Saloon, here seen on routine duty with a Grantham—Lincoln train near Peascliffe tunnel.

T. G. Hepburn. Rail Archive Stephenson

the growth of industry and population in the London Region and to encourage decentralisation. To this end some pretty unrealistic transport proposals were developed. They consisted mainly of general railway electrification within an area bounded by Didcot, Princes Risborough, Aylesbury, Watford, Luton, Hitchin, Bishop's Stortford, Chelmsford and Basingstoke, together with a new 'belt line' from Watford to Chelmsford, passing by Hemel Hempstead, Welwyn Garden City, Hertford, Ware, Harlow and (via a new railway) to Ongar, and then Margaretting on the GE Section.

Rather more realistic proposals (as one would expect from its membership) came from the Railway (London Plan) Committee appointed by the Minister of War Transport in February 1944 to look into the transport implications of the County of London Plan. This Committee was chaired by Professor Sir Charles Inglis and included among its members J. C. L. Train, Chief Engineer of the LNER, as well as Sir Eustace Missenden, General Manager of the Southern Railway.

Its proposals, submitted to the Minister in a Blue Book dated January 1946, proposed a network of new deep-level tunnels, some capable of taking trains of main line dimensions, crossing London and linking electrified services North and South of the Thames.

So far as the LNER was concerned, the chief proposal of interest was the rejection of most of

27. Hard work on the turntable – needed in steam days!

the Forshaw–Abercrombie proposals, and the suggestion of new routes in tunnel linking:

New Cross Gate (SR) and the Northern City Line (LPTB) connecting with the LNER suburban lines at Finsbury Park

North Kent East Junction (SR) to outside Marylebone, linking with Met & GC and GW and GC Joint lines

Loughborough Junction (SR) to near Finsbury Park, to link with LNER (GN) suburban services

A new freight tunnel, Loughborough Junction (SR) to Farringdon and the Metropolitan Widened Lines, for the LNER and the LMS.

These schemes were studied with mild interest; but at a time when even essential maintenance was still heavily in arrears they could hardly be considered very seriously.

The LNER might be bogged down on physical works, but grudging consent had been obtained from the Ministry to start overtaking the arrears of building passenger carriages. Much thought was devoted to the design of the post-war stock. A booklet entitled *Design for Comfort* outlined some questions confronting the carriage designer, such as open or compartment stock; single or two-piece doors to the corridor; single or twin luggage racks; and depth of windows. The booklet contained a tear-off questionnaire sheet and was widely distributed among passengers, the replies to the questionnaire being analysed at headquarters by Ness's staff.

Sir Charles Newton, the Chief General Manager, was deeply interested in design details and personally evolved a new layout to supersede the conventional one of external doors in the end vestibules, by placing the doors at the end of two intermediate cross-passages which effectively divided the compartments into three groups, thus shortening the distance between any individual compartment and the nearest exit door. Edward Thompson adopted the idea and the first post-war LNER vehicle became known as the 'Newton coach'.

Another novelty, largely developed in the Chief General Manager's office, was a new third-class sleeper with both double and single-berth compartments incorporating proper bedding and wash basins, in place of the austere 'lying-down accommodation' of the old four-berth third-class sleepers. Space was economised by an 'interlocking' design whereby adjacent compartments had upper berths superimposed on a lower berth next door, with a rebated partition preserving privacy. It was regrettable that this ingenious design, like a good many other LNER ideas, was dropped by British Railways after nationalisation.

7
Restoring Train Services, 1945–7

Sir Ronald Matthews was extremely anxious that the streamlined High Speed Trains should be restored as soon as possible after the end of the war: but the management warned him that the condition of the track, and the reliability of the locomotives after years of war service, made this impracticable for the time being. But on 1 October 1945, an average of 53 minutes was cut from the schedule of the day trains, eight in number, between King's Cross and Edinburgh, and an average of 36 minutes off the time of 14 trains between King's Cross and Newcastle. The down 'Flying Scotsman' now performed the journey in 7 hours 56 minutes.

However, as Cecil J. Allen reported sadly in the *Railway Magazine*, the condition of locomotives was making late arrivals far too frequent. A keen crew and the luck of the draw by having an engine in good shape were prerequisites for timekeeping. Even so, the Operating Superintendents and Locomotive Running Superintendents were determined to push on. On 21 and 22 May 1946 high-speed trials were undertaken between King's Cross and Edinburgh and back, in order to test the condition of the track at higher speeds than those hitherto in force. Line speeds for each section were prescribed, in addition to the normal local restrictions imposed by curvature or junctions. The locomotive was one of the original A4s – no. 2512, 'Silver Fox', with a 204-ton train. The actual running time to Edinburgh was 368 minutes northbound compared with the pre-war 354 minutes of the 'Coronation'; in view of the stops at Grantham, York and Newcastle, the trial trip was virtually at 'streamliner' speeds. In the up direction on the following day a speed of 102 mph was reached between Grantham and Peterborough; this news spread throughout the LNER and was a welcome tonic at a time when a return to pre-war standards seemed remote.

The excitement was short-lived, however, as the civil engineer imposed a number of speed restrictions pending track restoration to pre-war standards, and repetition of such high-speed running in regular services had to wait for some years. In fact, in 1947, after the shocking winter weather of 1946/7, 60 mph maximum speeds were reimposed over the LNER; but partial relaxations later in the year enabled better running performances to be achieved. Eventually

28. B2 no. 1671, 'Royal Sovereign', bursts out of Hadley Wood North tunnel with a Cambridge train in 1947.

F. R. Hebron. Rail Archive Stephenson

the LNER passed over to the Eastern, North Eastern and Scottish Regions of BR a fine tradition of fast running which has finally led to the era of modern High Speed Trains, the IC 125s of which Gresley would surely have approved.

Away from the East Coast Main Line, the Great Central route to London had come into its own, in a sense, in the latter stages of the war. From Sheffield, Nottingham, Loughborough and Leicester the competing Midland passenger train services were heavily loaded, often in fact overcrowded; delays were frequent owing to the heavy level of freight. The GC route, not so heavily used by freight south of Woodford, enjoyed in consequence considerable popularity with the business community. But the tradition inherited from the GCR of short, smartly-timed trains at frequent intervals could not survive. There appeared longer, slower trains of ten or more carriages upon which seats could usually be guaranteed. At stations with short island platforms such as Loughborough (which could only hold seven bogies) the length of trains often involved drawing up twice, with consequent delays.

One handicap on restoration of pre-war practices was the great wartime reduction in 'lodging turns', under which enginemen had to stay overnight away from home between turns of duty. In September 1939 these were drastically curtailed, partly because men were reluctant to be away from their families in view of the black-out and the threat of bombing produced feelings of insecurity in their families; partly because the end of long non-stop runs made the need for lodging turns less pressing. As O. S. Nock has written in *Locomotives of the LNER*,

In pre-war days a top-link King's Cross crew would take a Pacific engine from London to Newcastle, lodge the night, and then take the same locomotive back to London the next day; in all probability they would have the same engine for a week or more of heavy express duty. Under the wartime arrangement a crew would be required to take over a locomotive already 70 or 80 miles on its journey, work it for another 100 miles or so, and then hand over to a third crew . . . When an engine is in the hands of a pair of men for so short a time they cannot 'nurse' it as on a long journey, nor carry out the numerous small individual jobs which in the long run make all the difference to the sustained quality of locomotive performance.

There was resistance from the trade unions to the re-introduction of lodging turns, which never reappeared on the scale applicable before the war. Use of the former Great Central hotel, closed during the war and requisitioned by the War Office for a time, as a hostel for enginemen could only provide a temporary palliative effect in the case of men required to lodge in London.

The restoration of restaurant car services was very popular with the travelling public because, in times of continuing food rationing, eating out was an excellent way of augmenting one's diet! The menus available were restricted, though some of the more unpalatable wartime dishes of substitute materials, such as 'Woolton pie', disappeared. The 5s (25p) maximum price of meals, enforced by Government order, was still adequate to cover most though not all the costs of meal service. Local availability of supplies was a main factor, with restaurant cars in the Scottish Area seeming to have better contacts than those further south.

The LNER had had 58 Pullman cars on its system at the outbreak of war; in January 1939 the Board had agreed to renew the contract with Pullman, but only eight months later war conditions made it necessary to put the cars into storage. The LNER and the Southern Railway, it may be mentioned, jointly guaranteed the

29. A welcome break in post-war austerity; a crowd of visitors arrives at the new LNER station built for Butlin's Filey Holiday Camp, 1947.

National Railway Museum

53

30. A3 no. 55, 'Woolwinder', near Potters Bar with the reinstated 'Yorkshire Pullman'.

F. R. Hebron. Rail Archive Stephenson

Pullman Company £50,000 a year during the war as compensation for the loss of receipts consequent upon suspension of services.

Restoration of Pullman services after the war was slow but in 1946 the 'Yorkshire Pullman' reappeared; a touch of pre-war luxury that was much appreciated in the age of austerity. It was not until after nationalisation that something resembling the pre-war number of all-Pullman trains reappeared on the Eastern and North Eastern Regions of BR.

In the more humdrum field of commuter traffic, one small sign of a return to pre-war practice had been the restoration on 30 July 1945

of a limited service of passenger trains between LNER suburban stations and the LMS City terminus, Broad Street which, like nearby Moorgate, had been heavily bombed. There were, however, two important changes. The LMS North London trains had before the war worked only to Brookmans Park on the GN main line and Gordon Hill on the Hertford loop. The post-war service extended as far as Welwyn Garden City and Hertford North. And whereas LMS stock had previously been employed, now LNER eight-coach sets of two articulated 'quads' with N2 0–6–2T locomotives provided the service – the first LNER workings into and out of Broad Street.

54

8

To the Continent Again

Even before the outbreak of war, in August 1939, the Admiralty took over part of Parkeston Quay, and on 2 September the whole of the Harwich services ceased to operate, the masters of vessels in European ports being ordered to return home as quickly as possible.

Most of the railway-owned ships were immediately requisitioned for war service. The LNER's Harwich-based vessels were soon largely transferred to Southampton where they were first employed in transporting the British Expeditionary Force to the Continent. The ss *Prague*, during the Dunkirk evacuation, was heavily bombed with 3,000 French troops on board and had to be beached at Deal, but was afterwards salvaged and repaired. Later she became a hospital ship for the US Army in Europe, being returned to the LNER at the end of the war and reconverted to a passenger vessel for her old duties on the Hook night service.

Her sister ship, ss *Vienna*, was also engaged in the Dunkirk evacuation and was eventually purchased by the Government as a troop transport – a transaction which Robert Bell was reported to have concluded on his own responsibility and which was queried by some LNER Directors. The third ship from the Hook night service, ss *Amsterdam*, was lost; after taking part in the Dunkirk operation and troop-ing work in the Orkneys and Shetlands, she was turned into an infantry landing vessel and used as such for the Normandy landings, later becoming a hospital ship. In this capacity she was mined, and sank off the French coast in 1944.

From the older, ex-GER fleet, ss *St Denis* and ss *Malines* were sent to Rotterdam to evacuate British nationals upon the invasion of Holland. *St Denis* was caught at Rotterdam and had to be scuttled by her crew, who left on the last British destroyer to get away; *Malines* returned safely with 200 evacuees and soon afterwards took part in the Dunkirk operation, later becoming a naval escort vessel in the Mediterranean, where she was torpedoed off Alexandria, raised and repaired but found unfit for duty other than as a depot ship.

The ss *Bruges* was bombed and sunk in the evacuation from Le Havre in 1940. The ss *Antwerp* also served in the Mediterranean and in 1945 became a BAOR leave vessel. The ss *Archangel* was the fourth vessel from the ex-GER fleet to be a war casualty, being bombed and sunk in the North Sea off Aberdeen whilst on trooping service in 1941.

The three train ferries were at first kept in service carrying rail wagons, ambulance trains and military stores from Harwich to France. One of them, 'Train Ferry No. 2', was sunk at

31. Unusual Continental passengers; German prisoners of war being repatriated via the LNER.

St Valéry; the other two were bought by the Government, converted into assault landing craft and given fancy names by the Admiralty – perhaps thereby showing the naval contempt for civilian vessels? The new names were *Princess Iris* and *Princess Daffodil*. The last named was mined and sank in the English Channel in March 1945 whilst carrying locomotives for use on the Continent. *Princess Iris* was, however, bought back by the LNER in March 1946 and given a more suitably prosaic name for such a utilitarian vessel, *Essex Ferry*.

The ex-GCR fleet continued to sail between the Humber and the Continent until May 1940 when it too was requisitioned. The ss *Accrington*, ss *Bury*, ss *Dewsbury* and ss *Stockport* became convoy rescue ships, with the arduous duty of

32. King George Dock, Hull.

BBC Hulton Picture Library

picking up survivors from any ship in a convoy which might be torpedoed. *Stockport* was lost at sea in 1943.

The ss *Felixstowe* (a small ex-GER freighter of 882 gross tons) and *Bury* had both been at Antwerp at the time of the invasion and, more fortunate than the *St Denis* at Rotterdam, were able to steam down the river and escape in time.

The LNER's Marine Superintendent, Captain R. Davis, was released by the Company 'for the duration' and transferred to a post in charge of the Sea Transport department of the Ministry of War Transport. The Continental Traffic Manager, A. L. Gibson, retained his title pending the end of the war and the resumption of services; but on the retirement of C. J. Selway, who had been Passenger Manager of the Southern Area since the Grouping, 'ALG' took over this active post on 27 July 1940.

But the Continental Department had always

33. Parkeston Quay, Harwich, almost back to normal after the war.

BBC Hulton Picture Library

been known for esprit de corps and, despite a staff now widely scattered, on 20 February 1943 no less than 50 of the pre-war total of 80 were able to meet at a reunion lunch in a South Kensington hotel to renew personal contacts and, in speeches, to look forward to the post-war renewal of their work. Three Continental associates – J. Noest of the Zeeland Steamship Company, A. B. Cockell of Westcott and Co. of Antwerp, and A. Mertz of the Belgian Railways and Marine – were present as a symbol of the friendship that had always existed between the LNER Continental Department and its associates on the far side of the North Sea. Sadly, only ten months later, A. L. Gibson who had for so long been an outstanding LNER figure, died, on 24 December 1943. It was especially sad that he did not live to see the resumption of the LNER's links with Holland and in particular the restoration of personal contacts with the executives of the firm of Hudig and Peters, who had long been the LNER's agents at the Hook, some of whom had suffered much during the Nazi occupation.

The long-awaited resumption of the night Hook service took place in November 1945, but instead of three passenger ships only *Prague* was available; *Vienna* having been sold and now used as a War Office transport and *Amsterdam*, as mentioned above, having been lost. So the service started on a thrice-weekly basis. The train ferry to Zeebrugge also restarted with one ship, the *Essex Ferry* (pre-war 'Train Ferry No. 1').

Links with Denmark, too, were restored quickly; in the early part of 1946 the Danish United Steamship Company placed a large new vessel, the MS *Kronprinz Frederik* on the Harwich–Esbjerg service. The LNER restored the 'Scandinavian' boat train and, as in the case of the Hook route, a thrice-weekly service was established.

Later that year, on 7 November, the first post-war LNER ship for the Harwich–Hook service was launched – the ss *Arnhem* of 4,490 gross tons. The launching ceremony was performed by the wife of the Dutch ambassador, in the presence of the burgomaster of Arnhem. Delivered in the summer of 1947, the new ship was faster than any of her predecessors.

Arnhem was not actually the first ship to be built for the LNER after the war – that distinction belonged to the PS *Waverley* for the Clyde river services, launched at the yard of A. & J. Inglis in the Pointhouse shipyard on the Clyde, as a replacement for the earlier vessel of that name, sunk at Dunkirk during the evacuation.

A second train ferry, *Suffolk Ferry* was, however, launched on 7 May 1947 to help cope with the increased demand for the ferry services.

The Parkeston Quay–Antwerp service re-started in the summer of 1946 but after wartime losses the only available ships were ex-GCR ones – *Dewsbury* and *Accrington*, both of 1,678 gross tons – no match for the 4,220-ton *Prague* – and the Antwerp service failed to re-establish itself on a permanent basis.

However, even though ships were fewer and the service thinner than in pre-war times, it was a boost to LNER morale in those rather dreary days of post-war austerity, to see the 'Hook Continental' and the 'Scandy' once more pulling out of Liverpool Street. L. H. K. (Leo) Neil, formerly Gibson's Assistant, had returned from his wartime post as London City Manager to succeed Gibson, and a reactivated Continental Department began once more to be something which both the Board and the chief officers could regard with pride.

9
Major Schemes Restarted: the Woodhead Problem

Some parts of the 1935–40 New Works Programme had made good progress up to the outbreak of war, before work had to be suspended. By September 1939, on the Liverpool Street–Shenfield project two miles of overhead girder for the electric conductor wire had been erected; the Ilford steam locomotive depot had been demolished and preparations made for the new electric line layout.

The preliminary works for the flyover at Ilford had been started. It was designed to carry the local lines over the through lines between Manor Park and Ilford, this reversal of position being essential for the working of an intensive electric service into Liverpool Street. The main line platforms (nos 9 and 10) were in the centre of the station; but the through lines were on the north side which involved a degree of conflicting movement with the suburban services which, always a handicap, would be quite unacceptable once the electrification to Shenfield had been completed. The flyover was actually brought into use, though with steam trains using it for the time being, on 6 October 1947.

Contracts had also been placed before the war for the passenger coaches to be used on both the

Shenfield and the Manchester–Glossop local services – all-steel saloons with passenger-operated press-button door controls – but delivery had to wait until peace returned.

In the London area there had also been good progress with the 600-volt fourth-rail electrification for the lines to be operated by London Transport, including the site for the extension of Finsbury Park station to take the Northern City tube trains to Alexandra Palace – a scheme which was never carried out after the war, owing to revised estimates of likely traffic levels. By contrast, the work of projecting the LPTB Northern Line trains over the LNER High Barnet branch went on to completion, although the electrification to Edgware was postponed owing to war conditions and when work resumed after the war it was decided to cut the line short at Mill Hill East and abandon the remainder of the route.

So, on 14 April 1940, the tube trains started running to High Barnet from East Finchley, although the new intermediate tube station at Highgate, below the LNER station (still served by steam trains for the time being) did not open until the summer of that year.

On the Great Eastern section, progress had

60

34. The Ilford flyover, as it was at the beginning of the war.

Fox Photos

not been quite so advanced for the handover to London Transport. Work on the extensions of the Central Line eastward was abandoned early in 1940; but the new tunnels of the LPTB between Leytonstone and Newbury Park had reached a stage at which they could temporarily be used as a bomb-proof factory for the Plessey Company, then manufacturing important electronic equipment for the Forces.

Work soon resumed at the end of the war, and in December 1946 the Central Line tube trains reached Stratford, where there was cross-platform exchange with LNER steam trains, pending electrification. On 5 May 1947 London Transport was able to extend the Central Line trains as far as Leytonstone, passing through a new tube tunnel between Stratford and Leyton, where the LNER tracks were joined. The LNER steam suburban service between Liverpool Street, Loughton, Epping and Ongar was

61

H. C. Casserley

35. The new platforms at Stratford, awaiting electrification on 13 October 1945.

curtailed at Leytonstone, which became an exchange point with the tube trains. (The steam service was progressively cut back as the electrification progressed, though it was after nationalisation that Woodford and later Epping became the changeover points.)

In the bleak Pennines, on the Woodhead route, seven miles of overhead girders were in place by 1939 and the new electric locomotive depot at Darnall, near Sheffield, was under construction. Special overhead equipment was being installed in the Woodhead tunnel itself. But a major snag appeared when work was resumed. The condition of the three-mile bore had deteriorated during the war, when the

heavy freight traffic over the Woodhead route had increased to a new peak. The tunnel had always been dreaded by enginemen who, with a heavy freight on a rising gradient and the tunnel full of smoke from the previous train, could experience ten to fifteen minutes of near-asphyxiation. Even when free of choking smoke, the tunnel had a characteristic odour which Sir Ronald Matthews in a speech once compared to 'the flavour of cheap port – a beverage of which I am *not* a connoisseur.'

The extent to which the tunnel lining had deteriorated during the war gave the engineers concern, and Balfour Beatty and Co. were asked to report on the tunnel's condition. An inspection, in the company of the Chief Engineer, was

Fox Photos

36. An LNER steam train passes the first LPTB test electric train in Stratford station, 25 November 1946.

made on 18 March 1945 and in the following June a report was submitted to J. C. L. Train to the effect that

    . . . in all parts of the tunnel, whether dry or wet, the lime mortar has decomposed completely in the inside ring of lining . . . in the crown the blast from the locomotive chimneys has blown it out to a depth of 3–4 inches and where water is percolating through more has been washed out, the ring in places appearing to stand as a dry stone arch . . . Individual stones have fallen out . . . there is bulging of the vertical walls inward.

This alarming state of affairs could be remedied, the report suggested, in several ways. Enlargement of one of the two single-line bores to take double track, with relining, was estimated to cost £3.1 million. There were other options – relining the existing twin bores with cast-iron arches on new concrete sidewalls, relining throughout with aluminised cement or relining with cast-iron circular segments – all would involve serious interference with traffic for a long time. The best solution would be a new double-line tunnel, which would cost – depending on the lining selected – between £2.6 million and £3.1 million.

Train spoke to the Chief General Manager

63

37. Steam and electric side by side on the Central Line extension at Loughton.

and one or two other officers about the dilemma in which this report placed the LNER; but for the time being he refrained from reporting it to the Chairman. However, Sir Ronald in the early autumn of 1946 paid one of his semi-social, semi-official visits to 'The Hoo', staying overnight in the Chief General Manager's bungalow. In the course of conversation after dinner, Miles Beevor, the Chief Legal Adviser, asked Train what the position was about the new Woodhead tunnel. The cat was out of the bag! The Chairman immediately demanded to know what was afoot, somewhat to the discomfiture of the officers.

A costly project of this kind, and one which would not earn additional revenue, was a matter of concern to the Board. Sir Ronald required a second opinion and personally, together with the Chairman of the Board's Works Committee, met Sir William Halcrow, head of the distinguished consulting engineering firm, on 1 March 1946, commissioning a report which was produced, with commendable speed, on 17 April.

Halcrows confirmed the serious character of

64

38. Finchley Central, electrified since 1941.

B. Hardy

the bulging of the side walls and argued that temporary relining was only a palliative, though some of it must be done as a matter of urgency. Four alternative long-term solutions were examined, but a new double-line tunnel was considered the best option. Halcrows put the estimated cost at a lower figure than Balfour Beatty had done, namely at £1,820,000.

On 25 November 1947 the Works Committee approved the construction of the new Woodhead tunnel at an estimated cost of £2,282,000. Contracts, however, could not be let before nationalisation; and in the event the Railway Executive accepted the tender of Balfour Beatty & Co. at £2,318,919, after temporary remedial works had been carried out.

39. Approach to the Woodhead tunnel by steam, though with the electric wires already in place.

C. R. L. Coles

Had the closure of the Woodhead route by British Rail in 1981 been foreseen, one wonders what answer would have been found to the problem posed in 1945–7!

On a more cheerful note, reference must be made to the opening of the short new railway and station serving Butlin's holiday camp at Filey on the Yorkshire coast, in the summer of 1947. This was celebrated with junketings in great style, a special Pullman train from London bringing the guests who were regaled with a performance of 'La Bohème' in the camp theatre with famous Italian artists on stage. It helped one to forget, for a few hours, both the depressing effect of post-war austerity and the threat of nationalisation round the corner.

10
Gresley, Thompson and Peppercorn

The death of Sir Nigel Gresley on 5 April 1941, after a short illness, was a shock to everyone on the LNER because he had been so closely identified with the features that had most kept the LNER in the public eye. He had (unusually in his profession) for no less than 30 years held the chief executive position in the mechanical engineering function, first on the GNR and then the LNER. Of course, the last year and a half of his career had been clouded by wartime conditions. Being rather more of a design engineer than a workshops engineer, there was little scope after 1939 for exercising the chief talents he possessed, though he had always been a keen believer, as his obituary in the *Railway Magazine* mentioned, in 'making a point of moving about the line and inspecting his shops down to the minutest detail.' He certainly threw himself into supervising the conversion of the Dukinfield works for war purposes with special keenness.

It must have been gratifying to him also to receive reports on how well his Pacifics and (in particular) the V2 2–6–2s were coping in war-time with loads far beyond those they had been designed to haul. In the V2s, of which over 180

existed, he had a partial answer to those critics who pointed to the lack on the LNER of a large fleet of general-purpose mixed-traffic engines such as the LMS and the GWR possessed.

He may have had some reservations about the choice of a Stanier LMS 2–8–0 as the Ministry of Supply standard for military use; but the nearest LNER counterpart would have been the Robinson 2–8–0 design which, robust and successful as it had been when it was the ROD (Railway Operating Division) standard engine in 1914–18, dated from 1911 and was thus hardly a serious competitor.

During his lifetime Gresley was known for the locomotives he actually built; the general public knew nothing of those designs that had never got beyond the drawing board. Six years after Gresley's death one of his chief designing aides, B. Spencer, delivered a fascinating paper to the Institution of Locomotive Engineers which described a number of these abortive but interesting projects. One was for a 2–6–4T 2-cylinder engine for the GE Southend line services, to replace the rather elderly B12s; another for a 2–6–4T for the GN suburban services, and yet another, a 2–8–2T with three

National Railway Museum

40. Gresley's 'counter-pressure' locomotive, used for engine testing before completion of the Locomotive Testing Station at Rugby.

cylinders, for local mineral working in the Nottinghamshire coalfield. More striking were proposals for a 3-cylinder 4–8–2 design for heavy express passenger trains, and a 2–6–4–4 articulated engine-and-tender unit, a novel idea abandoned in favour of the more conventional V2 2–6–2 which proved so successful.

Later came the outlines of a new 3-cylinder 4–6–0 to replace both the K3 and B17 classes; a new 3-cylinder 2–6–0 rather similar to the K3 class; and yet another 2–6–4T with 5 ft 8 in. driving wheels intended to give high acceleration on suburban train services. This latter

might well have been included in a building programme had the war not intervened and effectively put a stop to these new projects in the mind of Sir Nigel, the 'designing man' as he had been described when presented for his honorary degree.

It was sad that Gresley did not live to see the realisation of a project especially dear to his heart, the establishment of a scientific loco-motive testing station. In June 1936 the CGM and Gresley had reported verbally to the Board's Locomotive Committee about the advantages of such a scheme, the notional cost being £160,000. The Committee decided that an approach should be made to the LMS to share in

41. Edward Thompson.

National Railway Museum

42. Arthur H. Peppercorn.

National Railway Museum

the project, and in June 1937 it was reported that agreement had been reached. The site would be Rugby; a Joint LNER/LMS Superintending Committee would be set up, and the cost, now estimated at £180,000, would be shared 50/50 between the two Companies.

In October 1939 it was decided, despite the outbreak of war, to let the contract for the building, but all equipment on order was to be stored 'for the duration'.

Pending the launching of this scheme, Gresley had used a counter-pressure locomotive. No. 761, an ex-NER B13 4–6–0, due for scrapping, had been altered so as 'to furnish the necessary resistance in the rear of the

dynamometer car when testing another engine.' The pistons, in other words, now absorbed the input of energy instead of transmitting energy to the driving wheels. They thus enabled the dynamometer car to calculate horsepower output from any engine under test. But the Rugby station was to provide much more refined data when it finally opened after the war and it would have delighted Gresley.

Gresley's death evoked many tributes, not merely to his achievements as a great locomotive designer but also to his personality. 'A great Englishman, whose ancestors fought at Agincourt,' wrote Sir Ralph Wedgwood. 'He was a good talker and capital company on the

69

43. The ungainly lines of Thompson's rebuilding of Gresley's classic A1.

44. *(upper right)* A contrast: the fine proportions of Thompson's own B1 design.

45. *(right)* A2/3 no. 500, 'Edward Thompson', on shed at Doncaster, June 1946.

dullest day . . . he was almost boisterously fond of country life.'

He was buried at Netherseale in Derbyshire, where his father had been rector for many years, on the same day that a memorial service for him was held in Chelsea Old Church – just a week before the old church was demolished in an air raid. Watton House, his country home, for a time became an LNER training school.

Gresley's successor, Edward Thompson, was in temperament a very different person. He was rather more academic an engineer than Gresley, having taken the Mechanical Sciences Tripos at Cambridge at an age when Gresley was gaining practical experience as an engineering pupil in Horwich works. Slim, clean-shaven and austere in appearance, 'ET' was privately known in some top echelons of the LNER as 'Dead Ned' – a nickname that was rather unfair to a very capable engineer. But it was no secret on the

LNER that he and Gresley had disagreed on various issues, and it also seemed at times that this was a struggle between Great Northern and North Eastern traditions.

If so, it was a pity. The founding fathers had gone to considerable lengths to prevent pre-Grouping rivalries from prejudicing the emergence of the LNER as a true entity, and in the traffic and civil engineering functions this had paid off. But in mechanical engineering it seemed more difficult to prevent clashes between Doncaster and Darlington.

Edward Thompson, it happened, was also a son-in-law of Sir Vincent Raven. Even apart

British Rail

T. G. Hepburn. Rail Archive Stephenson

46. Another neat and well-proportioned Thompson design, the L1 2–6–4T.

from this, on his own merits, he could have expected to succeed as CME of the North Eastern Railway at one remove from Raven, after A. C. Stamer had held the post, had the Grouping not intervened. Frustration in this respect could have left him with a trace of bitterness.

Thompson's North Eastern loyalties, surviving the long period of Doncaster dominance, faintly echoed what Crewe had suffered on the LMS during the period of Derby dictatorship of locomotive policy. These loyalties even seemed to emerge in some rather trivial ways, as when Thompson during the war replaced the initials 'LNER' with 'NE' on locomotive tender and tank sides – ostensibly on the grounds of economy!

At the time of Gresley's death Thompson was Mechanical Engineer of the GN and GC sections of the Southern Area; he was, in fact, much more of a workshops man than his late chief, having had charge, through a succession of appointments during various periods between 1912 and 1941, of all the LNER's main locomotive, carriage and wagon works in England – Doncaster, York, Darlington, Shildon, Stratford and Gorton. He was very interested in progressive repair systems and workshop productivity.

It may be mentioned here that after Gresley's death the Board decided to detach electrical engineering from the CME's department and appointed H. W. H. Richards as the LNER's first Chief Electrical Engineer as an all-line departmental officer in his own right. Richards

T. G. Hepburn. Rail Archive Stephenson

47. One perhaps surprising result of Edward Thompson's standardisation policy: rebuilding of ex-GCR 0–6–0 class J11/3 no. 4318 seen at Nottingham (Victoria), May 1947.

had joined the LB&SCR in 1913 and had become Assistant Electrical Engineer on the Southern Railway before joining Gresley in 1924. Richards's appointment by the Board obviously looked forward to the post-war completion of both the Liverpool Street–Shenfield and the Manchester–Sheffield–Wath electrification schemes.

During the war Edward Thompson was heavily occupied with keeping the traffic departments as well supplied with motive power as current restrictions would permit, as well as overseeing the many new commitments of the railway shops – work for other railways and for the Ministry of Supply competing with the LNER's own needs. But before long the three main facets of his own locomotive policy began to emerge: these were, first, production of reliable mixed-traffic locomotives of straight-

73

48. Gresley's original P2, 'Cock o' the North', as finally rebuilt.

National Railway Museum

forward design, and thus low maintenance costs; secondly, extensive rebuilding of Gresley's three-cylinder locomotives to eliminate the conjugated valve gear; lastly, the production of a standardisation and renumbering scheme for the whole LNER stock.

The first-fruits appeared as early as 1942, when the prototype of Thompson's B1 4–6–0 class was built. Named 'Springbok', it was the forerunner of the Antelope class designed for mixed-traffic work, a workman-like two-cylinder design with a round-topped firebox and a nominal tractive effort of only 26,878 lb compared with the 33,730 lb of Gresley's V2 design.

The choice of two cylinders was dictated by the need for simplicity that would keep down both the first cost and the maintenance costs. In the case of the latter, it was not merely finance but the availability of skilled labour and shop floor space that needed to be economised under wartime and post-war conditions – con-

siderations that later on were to weigh heavily with R. A. Riddles after nationalisation when the BR standard steam locomotives were being designed.

Over 200 B1s were built between 1942 and 1946 and these useful machines undoubtedly served the LNER well, if unspectacularly, at a difficult time. Thompson made a start on standardisation by using, in the B1 class, the wheel centres of the V2 and the boilers of the B17 classes. The B1 class produced a lower hammer-blow effect on the track – an important factor on the Great Eastern Section – compared with the B17 (Sandringham) class which Gresley had built for the GE from 1928: their route availability was thus very wide indeed.

The next Thompson design was the L1 2–6–4T for both passenger and freight work, including semi-fast and suburban passenger duties. The prototype L1 performed very well – its tractive effort of 32,081 lb was well above that of the B1 – and Thompson intended that no

49. A. H. Peppercorn and his staff, 31 December 1947.

National Railway Museum

less than 1,000 should ultimately be built under his standardisation policy. This, however, was not to be under nationalisation.

The second aspect of Thompson's policy was perhaps the most controversial one, namely, the elimination of Gresley's favourite form of 'conjugated' valve gear. Thompson harped upon the weakness of the motion for the middle cylinder being derived from the 'two-to-one lever' in a report to the Locomotive Committee of the Board, so much so that Sir Ronald Matthews was once heard to say, 'We really cannot build a locomotive policy for the LNER on the basis that everything Gresley did was wrong.'

But it certainly seemed to be the case that excessive play developed in the linkage after heavy wear and inadequate maintenance, as was the case during the war years, and Thompson obtained authority to make a start with re-building Gresley's famous Pacifics. The original GNR A1 was rebuilt with three sets of Walschaerts valve gear for each cylinder, a boiler pressure of 250 lb and an ungainly appearance compared with the elegance of Gresley's 1922 design. (In fact, people were struck by the contrast between the neatness of Thompson's own designs and the apparently deliberate 'uglification' of Gresley engines.) Thompson proposed to rebuild on the same lines all Gresley's A1 Pacifics, now reclassified as A10.

Thompson reconstructed the P2 (2–8–2) class as Pacifics, classed A2/2, and started to modify the V2 (2–6–2) engines in the form of a new Pacific classed A2/1. Finally, he produced his own new Pacific class, A2/3, also with the high boiler pressure of 250 lb helping to give it a tractive effort of 40,430 lb.

The impression that Thompson was denigrating his predecessor's designs was not entirely removed by a study of his standardisation plan. This, he claimed, was not a rigid, predetermined programme, but an attempt to reduce markedly the number of locomotive classes to be maintained in traffic. Three groups were prescribed: the first to include nine or ten new standard types, the only classes to be built in future, until a demand should arise for new classes for purposes that the existing stock could

75

not meet adequately; the second to include types which were not to be built further, but which were worth maintaining until the end of their useful life, being reboilered if necessary; the third to include all the other locomotives in the LNER fleet, which would normally be scrapped as and when boilers could no longer be found for them from stock.

The standard classes comprised the two Thompson rebuilds of Gresley engines, comprising the A1 (6 ft 8 in. driving wheels) and A2 (6 ft 2 in. driving wheels) Pacifics and, of course, Thompson's own A2/3. Next came the Thompson B1 4–6–0, and a new K1 2–6–0 in the form of a rebuild of Gresley's K4 for the West Highland line. The heavy mineral class was to be supplied by a Thompson rebuild of a Robinson 01 2–8–0 and a Gresley 02. For lighter freight work, Robinson's J11 0–6–0, as rebuilt by Thompson, was selected. The mixed-traffic tank type was to be Thompson's L1 2–6–4; and for shunting work, rebuilt versions of a Robinson Q1 0–8–0T and Gresley's J50 0–6–0T were chosen.

It was noteworthy that Gresley's A3 and A4 Pacifics were only to be maintained, not perpetuated. It was also interesting to note the age of some of the Robinson types selected for rebuilding. The O1 design went back to 1911, the Q1 to 1902, and the J11 to 1901. This was a tribute to their remarkable strength, especially in the main frames, something which Robinson had always provided in his engines.

Like many standardisers, Edward Thompson did not remain in office long enough to see his policy carried fully into effect, as he retired on 30 June 1946. A month earlier, a graceful tribute had been paid to him by naming an A2 Pacific (no. 500, under the new numbering scheme which he had instigated) 'Edward Thompson'. It was, incidentally, the 2,000th locomotive to be built in the Doncaster Plant Works.

Thompson's successor, Arthur H. Peppercorn, was temperamentally much more akin to the extrovert Gresley than to his immediate predecessor. 'Peps', as he was widely known, was a genial character who had been closely associated with Gresley; but he was to have only eighteen months in office as the LNER CME before nationalisation. One of his first moves, which greatly cheered many at Doncaster, was to recall to design work some of Gresley's former assistants, notably B. Spencer.

He inherited from Edward Thompson the prototype rebuild of the Gresley three-cylinder K4 2–6–0 now classed K1. Peppercorn put production in motion and eventually 70 more were built. He also continued the building of Thompson B1s and L1s; but he stopped the construction of Thompson's A2/2 mixed-traffic Pacific after the original order for fourteen had been completed.

Peppercorn then produced his own Pacific with 6 ft 2 in. driving wheels; this retained the three sets of Walschaerts valve gear – perhaps a tacit admission that in this respect Thompson had been right! – but the general appearance was more akin to the classic elegance of Gresley than that of the Thompson rebuilds. It emerged from shops just in time to have 'LNER' rather than 'British Railways' painted on its tender, and it was named 'A. H. Peppercorn', in accordance with a pleasant custom that had grown up on the LNER.

On 1 January 1948 Peppercorn became responsible to his new ex-LMS chief, R. A. Riddles, at the Railway Executive. Even though his more easy-going temperament did not rebel as strongly against the new organisation as did, for example, Gresley's former Assistant Oliver Bulleid, now CME of the Southern, Peppercorn retired at the end of 1949 after only two years' experience of the new, LMS-dominated regime. Sadly, he died on 3 March 1951.

11
East Coast and other Diesels

Both Gresley and Peppercorn were associated to some extent with diesel traction, though Edward Thompson seems to have had relatively little interest in its possibilities. Gresley was certainly a steam engineer by training and outlook; but his receptive mind was always interested in new possibilities, though the LNER's shortage of capital resources imposed sharp limits on speculative schemes. He readily co-operated in trials of manufacturers' experimental prototypes, such as the Kitson-Still diesel-steam locomotive which was tested in the North Eastern Area, and the later trials of a 240 hp Ganz railcar in the same Area.

The North Eastern Area was very much in the lead where diesel railcar proposals were concerned, largely because of its number of lightly-loaded branch and secondary passenger services where economies could be obtained if conventional trains were replaced by railcars. Originally these were, of course, steam units, no less than 50 of which were authorised for purchase by the Locomotive Committee on 28 July 1927; but in March 1932 the Locomotive Committee was told of the successful trial of a 250 hp oil-electric railcar supplied by Sir W. G. Armstrong Whitworth & Co. After

further trials this unit was bought for £7,500. In April 1934 two more such units were acquired, for a total of £11,000. There were, however, maintenance problems with these three railcars, named 'Tyneside Venturer', 'Lady Hamilton' and 'Northumbrian'; and on 7 November 1936 the Divisional General Manager of the North Eastern Area, Jenkin Jones, wrote to his Superintendent and Locomotive Running Superintendent as follows. 'I understand that the Chief Mechanical Engineer has come to the conclusion that it is no use repairing the Diesel coaches unless we can find slow services on which they can operate in a steady-going fashion.' The outlook for diesel-mechanical railcars however seemed brighter and 'JJ's' letter continued: 'The Chief Mechanical Engineer thinks it might be possible to meet our requirements by means of a coach on the Great Western pattern worked by two AEC omnibus engines.'

Meanwhile a 60-seater light diesel-electric railbus, also supplied by Armstrong Whitworth, had been bought for £2,500 in June 1934 and reports on its performance were made to the Locomotive Committee in the following year.

The war period prevented any development

77

50. One of the LNER's shunting diesels at March in 1946.

of 'JJ's' interest in diesel-mechanical railcars, but this revived in 1947 with a letter to his departmental officers suggesting that 57 diesel railcars and nine trailers could replace steam push-and-pull units with a saving provisionally estimated at £105,000 a year. The GWR experience in this field, 'JJ' requested, should be given particular study. This project led to a large volume of correspondence but did not reach the stage of a submission through the Chief General Manager to the Locomotive Committee before nationalisation killed it.

In the field of diesel shunters, the first step appears to have been the extended trials in 1932 of a six-coupled diesel-electric locomotive from Armstrong Whitworth. This led to a modest investment in diesel-electric shunters, and by 1947 four of them were working successfully in Whitemoor Yard. So, in this field the LNER experience followed that of the LMS, which had already decided that no more steam shunting

engines would be built, though on a more modest scale.

The main interest, of course, centres upon the extent to which diesel traction was considered for main line locomotives. On 28 July 1928 the Locomotive Committee agreed to a proposal from Gresley to purchase a diesel motor from Beardmores and an electric generator and control gear from the English Electric Company in order to convert an unspecified electric locomotive, surplus to traffic requirements, to diesel-electric traction. The estimated cost was £11,571.

Gresley's idea was that one of the Newport–Shildon Bo-Bo locomotives, converted in this way, could be employed on the heavy coal trains between Peterborough (New England yard) and London (Ferme Park), and could provide valuable data on the economics of the new form of traction. Unfortunately the contractors developed cold feet as to the feasibility of the project, especially over the power output required from the diesel motor and the modifications necessary to accommodate a larger

T. G. Hepburn. Rail Archive Stephenson

51. B1 no. 1141 leaving Wilford Bridge near Nottingham with a Cleethorpes–Leicester train in August 1947.

engine on the main frame. The scheme thus lapsed, the Locomotive Committee minuting on 28 November 1929 'no further action to be taken.'

After the end of the war, the LNER Board dispatched H. W. H. Richards to the USA in connection with the review of post-war policy being undertaken by all four main line railways. Richards reported on traction developments in North America and suggested that a substantial

trial of main line diesel traction might be now undertaken. Nothing particular in the form of action followed this report, nor after another report to the Locomotive Committee on 20 February 1947 from the Chief Mechanical Engineer and the Chief Electrical Engineer describing the principle of gas turbine-electric locomotives, with details of the (then) only working example, a Brown Boveri unit running trials on the Swiss Federal Railways. The report also referred briefly to the concept of a coal-

52. Austerity WD 77370 passing Red Hall, near Hatfield, with an up goods in 1947.

F. R. Hebron. Rail Archive Stephenson

burning gas turbine and outlined some of the problems involved. The authors seem to have been unaware of the GWR interest in gas turbines.

The Locomotive Committee took no specific action but resolved 'a comprehensive report dealing with all the various alternative traction methods to be submitted.' However, it was the Government's instruction, in the early part of 1947, to convert a number of locomotives from coal to oil fuel, that actually started the wheels turning. The fuel crisis of the hard winter of 1946/7 led the Government to tell the railways, through the REC, quickly to prepare coal-oil conversion schemes at Government expense. The LNER participation in this hasty and ill-considered measure involved an outlay of over £500,000.

During the period when the depots were being constructed and equipment for the locomotives manufactured, the point was put to me very forcibly that whereas a ton of fuel oil burnt in a locomotive firebox would save 1½ tons of coal, the same quantity of diesel oil used in a modern diesel locomotive would save five tons of coal.

I wrote a memorandum stressing this point and the suitability of the East Coast Main Line for a major trial of diesel traction, to Charles Hopkins, then Assistant General Manager (Traffic and Statistics). 'CPH' picked up the issue with enthusiasm and the Chief General Manager's office gathered the relevant departmental officers together in the preparation of an East Coast diesel scheme.

In July 1947 the Board's Joint Locomotive and Traffic Committee considered an important memorandum signed by the Chief General Manager, Miles Beevor, but mainly drafted by Hopkins, setting out the background, the justification and the details of the project. The Board approved the proposal to purchase 25 diesel-electric main line locomotives to replace 32 steam Pacifics, together with the construction of maintenance depots in Edinburgh and London, at a total cost of £1,390,000. Invitations were issued to suitable contractors to submit designs and quotations.

On 12 November tenders from six contractors were opened in the presence of Sir Ronald Matthews. Delivery dates for the first locomotive varied from 18 months to three years. With only six weeks to go before nationalisation, however, and under the restrictions enforced by the Transport Act 1947, the Board were unable to place an order; but the tenders were referred to the Railway Executive which took over on 1 January. The project dropped like a stone.

In the light of later events, the precipitate scrapping of the East Coast diesel scheme can be seen as nothing less than a tragedy, indirectly responsible for the disorderly scramble to get into diesel traction in the late 1950s and early 1960s. The LNER scheme would undoubtedly have run into teething troubles; but sorting these out would have provided an invaluable fund of experience upon which later diesel policy could be built. And the insistence in the LNER plan that proper maintenance facilities must be provided well in advance of the first locomotive being delivered was too often overlooked in BR days with serious consequences.

In view of its historic significance, the text of the memorandum to the LNER Board is printed as Appendix II though without the supporting details (which cover many pages) of the specification for the maintenance facilities, and full financial effects of the proposal. Reading it should dispose of any suggestion that the LNER scheme was hasty or ill-prepared, and should also highlight the responsibility of those who consigned it to the dustbin in no. 222 Marylebone Road!

12
Management After the War

The LNER had entered the war period with a Chairman and a Chief General Manager, neither of whom had been very long in office. The next six years were to see the retirement or death of a number of figures that had been prominent during the Whitelaw/Wedgwood period. C. J. Brown, the Engineer (Southern Area) and James Calder, who had been General Manager (Scotland) both died early in the war. C. J. Selway retired as Passenger Manager, Southern Area, on 27 July 1940, and H. H. Mauldin ('The Colonel') died less than a year later, at the early age of 58; the Southern Area was shocked at the loss of its Divisional General Manager after only three years in office. He was succeeded by George Mills, who retired in 1945.

G. Sutherland, the Chief Accountant, died in 1942 and was succeeded by L. C. Glenister. Robert Bell, for so long the 'grey eminence' of the LNER, retired in May 1943. He had not been able to recreate with Newton the special relationship he had had with Wedgwood; as the doyen of LNER management he had possessed a knowledge and an influence which Newton was bound to feel somewhat hampering to his own exercise of authority, even though the courtesies were always preserved, both men having a strong sense of propriety.

In November 1945 the Chief General Manager's office returned to London – not to the King's Cross premises which were out of action through bomb damage, but to a couple of houses in Dorset Square, just round the corner from Marylebone station which still housed the Chairman, Board Room and Secretary's office.

Sir Charles Newton had grown in stature since he had succeeded to the top job, when he must originally have found it a struggle to hold his own with such outstanding personalities as Lord Stamp and Sir James Milne. He was now a potentate, even though the strongly decentralised organisation of the LNER, with the power it gave to the three Divisional General Managers in Liverpool Street, York and Edinburgh, made policy formation rather difficult. The CGM was often in the position of a Roman charioteer driving a team of three horses, one of which would almost always be breaking away from the other two.

Newton was a strong supporter of standardisation even in such details as the design of lengthmen's huts and the position of the hot and cold taps in the hotel wash-basins. His ingenious mind led him to a less successful project, a universal ticket printing machine – a somewhat Heath-Robinsonian contraption, based upon the use of gear-wheels and chains and which lurked in an unfinished state beneath wrappings in a corner of the CGM's imposing office in Dorset Square. A tolerant CME had provided workshop assistance to build a prototype but the design problems were never solved.

He was able to pursue these interesting objectives unopposed, but the 'three emperors' strongly resisted any moves by the CGM that seemed seriously to threaten their prerogatives. They were particularly sensitive on this score because of wartime events. The civil engineering function had in 1942 been removed from their control and placed under an all-line officer, J. C. L. Train, the first Chief Engineer for the whole system. And war conditions had made it necessary to appoint an Assistant General Manager (Operating) for the whole system to represent the LNER on the Railway Executive Committee's Operating Committee and co-ordinate both inter-Area movement and rolling stock control on a unified basis. The DGMs had disliked this and had been only slightly mollified by adding the word 'Temporary' to the title of AGM (Operating) given to V. M. Barrington-Ward.

But despite this apparent move towards more central control, Sir Ronald Matthews and the Board continued to believe in the principle of decentralisation, though Newton (perhaps from his 19 years spent on the Great Western Railway) and Kenelm Kerr, the Assistant General Manager (Staff) did not entirely share their enthusiasm. 'KK', in fact, expressed his feelings by producing a highly contentious scheme for a centralised form of organisation, based upon departmental officers in all functions who would report direct to the CGM. This explosive document had to be kept under lock and key, as it ran counter to all the traditions of the railway, although it did however reflect in some ways Wedgwood's original ideas for the LNER,

which had not found favour with the Board in 1922–3.

As it was, in the Areas the 'three emperors' were all strong personalities, confident in their assumption that it was they who really ran the railway. T. F. Cameron was the lugubrious but shrewd and capable DGM in Edinburgh; C. M. Jenkin Jones, a razor-edge intellect and dominating personality, ruled in York; and the Southern Area was managed by the ebullient George Mills, whose background was mainly commercial.

Jenkin Jones (inevitably known everywhere as 'JJ') was a remarkable personality and had his health been better he would certainly have succeeded Newton as CGM. He did not suffer fools gladly, though he could exert great charm when he wished. An operating expert, he had been all-line Rolling Stock Controller and during the war had been entrusted with a special investigation into the GWR difficulties in handling the heavy wartime traffics in South Wales. His criticisms of GWR operating practices had deeply wounded Paddington, where the officers could hardly mention 'JJ' without exploding.

The contrast between 'JJ' and the DGM, Southern Area, was marked. George Mills was a skilful politician and diplomat with long experience of difficult commercial negotiations. His hobby was mountaineering, which led 'JJ' to devote a 'clerihew' to his brother officer, which ran:

> George Mills
> Climbs hills;
> In fact, the old devil
> Is very seldom on the level.

The views of an operator upon his commercial colleague could hardly be put more neatly. A. J. White, the highly intellectual

Courtesy C. S. McLeod

53. Robert Bell, the last of the true 'founding fathers' of the LNER.

Advertising Manager, once summed up the contrast rather more politely by the epigram: 'the operators play draughts; but the commercial men play chess.'

As nationalisation approached, there were

54. A2/3 no. 522, 'Straight Deal', approaching Grantham with a down express in 1947.

major changes in the top posts. George Mills was succeeded by V. M. Barrington-Ward, whose taciturnity was in startling contrast to the habits of his predecessor. In the Chief General Manager's office two rising stars were for a time nominally subordinate to O. H. Corble, the Assistant General Manager (Ancillary Services), but they soon emerged as fully-fledged AGMs in their own right. They were C. P. Hopkins, whose responsibilities were defined as Traffic and Statistics; and James Ness, covering the Works and General Sections.

Hopkins was, on nationalisation, to become Chief Regional Officer of the North Eastern Region of BR, at York; moving after a couple of years to Waterloo, first as Chief Regional Officer and then General Manager of the Southern Region. Ness became Chief Officer (New Works) of the Railway Executive, moving later to Scotland and eventually becoming General Manager, Scottish Region, and lastly a Member of the British Railways Board under Dr Beeching.

Sir Charles Newton used to refer with some complacency to the abilities of his two Assistants, whilst the Chairman – perhaps with a touch of gentle malice, since the term did not exactly delight the parties concerned – would speak of 'Castor and Pollux' or the 'heavenly

T. G. Hepburn. Rail Archive Stephenson

twins'. In fact, Sir Ronald's wit sometimes flowered into verses about the railwaymen he encountered: memory recalls one line,

'The sparkle of Arkle, the finesse of Ness'

which well captured the characters of the individuals named. (The brilliant Edward Arkle was at that time Goods Manager, Scottish Area: he held various important positions after nationalisation.)

The tradition of appointing relatively young men to important posts was deep-rooted on the LNER. It had been favoured by two influences – the career planning controlled by Robert Bell, and the decentralised Area organisation, which provided more departmental headships than could exist on a more centralised line and gave additional ladders of promotion. The three Areas were roughly weighted 5:3:2 and there was, therefore, the prospect that a young Passenger Manager, for instance, in the Scottish Area could move successively to York and then to Liverpool Street before reaching the top of the tree.

On 6 June 1947 Sir Charles Newton retired and was elected a Director of the LNER – a distinction which gave him great pleasure, even though it could only last a few months, with nationalisation just round the corner.

The Board's choice of a successor, failing Jenkin Jones, was the Chief Legal Adviser, Miles Beevor, who had joined the LNER in 1943. The selection of a lawyer for the top managerial post followed several happy precedents – the NER had had Sir George Gibb and Sir A. Kaye Butterworth, the Midland Sir Guy Granet – but Beevor had little time in which to prove himself. The Minister of Transport would only agree to an acting appointment; and before long, Beevor's nomination to the post of Chief Secretary and Legal Adviser to the future British Transport Commission involved him in spending his mornings running the LNER and his afternoons in attendance on the 'shadow' Commission – a situation little to his liking.

To study the LNER directory for the year 1947 is a revealing exercise. Out in the field there was a wealth of talent – chosen and fostered by 'RB' – which was to rise to high positions on British Rail in later years. To select names for mention is difficult and could be invidious; but the attempt must be made.

In the Southern Area, under Eric Rostern as Superintendent, there were the astute H. C. (Bill) Johnson, covering the GN/GC Sections – a future Chairman of British Rail – and for the GE Section Alex Dunbar (future Member of the British Railways Board). Out in the Districts were Gerard Fiennes at Stratford (future General Manager, Eastern Region) and Gordon Stewart (future GM, Scottish Region). In the Goods Manager's office under the redoubtable W. McAulay Gracie were A. A. Harrison and Donald Murray – both destined to reach high office.

At York, under E. M. Rutter as Superintendent, there was Lance Ibbotson (future General Manager of the Western and Southern Regions) and the Assistant Passenger Manager, Sidney Finnis who was, like A. E. H. Brown, Assistant DGM at Liverpool Street, to die tragically young after attaining the highest office in the nationalised Docks and Inland Waterways Executive.

In Scotland F. C. Margetts (Assistant Superintendent) was a future Member of the British Railways Board and Charles McLeod (Assistant Divisional General Manager) a future Chief Industrial Relations Officer.

The list could be extended almost indefinitely, but the message is clear enough. To have worked alongside or under such fine railwaymen was an experience and a privilege.

13
The Fight Against Nationalisation – and the End

On the morning of 6 July 1947 at lunchtime I walked into the Assistant Officers' room at 'The Hoo' and asked casually, 'How are the election results showing?' 'Very badly', was the answer. Suddenly everyone in the room had realised that nationalisation was not just an idea mooted by politicians, but something likely to affect all our lives.

Perhaps there was a subtle difference in attitudes between, on the one hand, the LNER Board of Directors and certain senior officers close to retirement; and on the other hand, the younger officers whose careers would have to continue under nationalisation. There was also perhaps a certain difference between the LNER and the other Companies, because William Whitelaw had in 1933 upset his brother Chairmen by stating in a public address that 'national ownership, with management completely divorced from political influence, is not impossible, and cannot be dismissed from consideration for all time because of the prejudice attached to the name of nationalisation.'

He had repeated these views elsewhere, no doubt because he was acutely conscious of the LNER's chronic shortage of capital for major improvements.

However, Sir Ronald Matthews was a strong Conservative and the LNER Board now, like the other Companies, decided to have no truck with the enemy, in the sense of discussing with the Minister of Transport the ways and means of giving effect to the Government's declared intention of nationalising the railways along with the other forms of public inland transport.

The four Chairmen, in the Railway Companies Association, started to dictate the strategy of a nation-wide campaign against nationalisation. The tactics were entrusted to a junior body comprising K. W. C. Grand, Assistant General Manager, GWR; John Elliot, Assistant General Manager, SR; A. J. Pearson, Assistant to President, LMS; and myself. An expensive public relations adviser from outside the industry was also engaged.

Pamphlets and leaflets were printed, setting out the railways' record in war and peace, and

55. 'The Aberdeen Fish' – A2/2 no. 503, 'Lord President', near St Fort.

Gavin L. Wilson

answering criticisms. We also launched a poster campaign, once the nationalisation Bill was on the way; the slogan was 'Stop the Transport Bill' to which I added, immediately after the coal crisis of 1946–7, 'You've just had one crisis; do you want another?'

It must be remembered that the railways at this time were still under Government control. We had to be very careful that all expenditure on opposing Government policy was kept out of the Government Control Account and was met from other funds owned by the shareholders.

Privately, some of us felt that the chances of success were non-existent, and that the best course would be to try to ensure that the future

organisation was a sensible one. But, of course, the attitude taken up by the Chairmen meant that the experience of practical railwaymen could not be made available to the civil servants engaged in drafting the Transport Bill. Had that been possible, perhaps the form of the future Railway Executive and its relationship to the British Transport Commission would have been better than proved to be the case between 1948 and 1953.

The railways found an ally in the fight against nationalisation in the Road Haulage Association. Under the common threat, road and rail produced a scheme of co-existence described in a joint statement, 'Co-ordination of Road and Rail Freight Transport'. The first real prospect

56. V2 no. 3650 arriving at Nottingham (Victoria) in August 1946.

T. G. Hepburn. Rail Archive Stephenson

of such co-operation had flowed from the railway 'Square Deal' campaign just before the war, when road and rail came close to settling their differences without Government intervention.

But the policy of the Attlee Government – steam-rollering vast measures of social and economic change through Parliament as quickly as possible – was singularly unresponsive to such ideas. I came to the conclusion that the only hope of influencing Whitehall would be through submitting alternative proposals which could fit inside the general framework of Government policy. I therefore drafted a paper proposing a 'mixed' transport organisation including public and private ownership. The railway Boards and managements would continue but would sell their track, signalling and structures to the State. They would then be granted a franchise to operate with their own locomotives, rolling stock, etc. For management purposes a federal British Railways Board would co-ordinate their activities.

Both the railway infrastructure and the national highway system, together with canals, ports and harbours, would be vested in a National Transport Authority which would be the supreme controller of investment and the

W. Philip Conolly

57. Spirit of the GN main line – A3 no. 63, 'Isinglass', breasting the Potters Bar summit.

recipient of the rentals paid for use of the infrastructure as well as of highway taxation.

There had been precedents for public ownership of railway infrastructure, coupled with railway operation by private enterprise, in France, Italy and India. I hoped that if the LNER Board could sell this concept to the Railway Companies Association, the latter might be able to sell it to the Minister. However, when I put it to the CGM, Sir Charles Newton felt that it was too radical a concept for the Board and he directed me instead to work on his own more limited project known as the 'landlord and tenant' scheme. This also involved the sale of the infrastructure to the Government but omitted all ideas of a central British Railways Board and of a National Transport Authority.

I accordingly drafted a paper entitled 'The State and the Railways', which the LNER Board accepted and described as 'An Alternative to Nationalisation' – not the wisest of titles from

58. York station on a typical afternoon.

the selling angle. It seemed for a time that the LMS would join with the LNER in advocating the 'landlord and tenant' scheme, and had the two biggest Companies agreed they could probably have swayed the remainder. However, at the last minute the Chairman of the LMS changed his mind and the LNER were faced with the choice of dropping their scheme or going it alone. They chose the latter course and 'The State and the Railways' was launched in a somewhat half-hearted way at a press conference of which one newspaper reported rather unkindly that Sir Ronald was supported only by 'a row of glum executives'. The scheme, when submitted formally to the Minister of Transport, was dismissed by that dignitary in a single sentence.

With less than five months to go before vesting day, the atmosphere became strained and artificial. On the one hand, the LNER Board

---

THE STATE
AND
THE RAILWAYS

AN ALTERNATIVE
TO
NATIONALISATION

Memorandum by the Board of the London
and North Eastern Railway Company

October, 1946

Author's Collection

59. The LNER's bid to survive.

continued to function, authorising new works and approving appointments; on the other, the officers were wondering where their future would lie. Barrington-Ward and Train were sent for by the Minister and offered appointments, which they accepted, as Members of the future Railway Executive. Newton had retired and the new CGM, Miles Beevor (Chief Secretary and Legal Adviser-designate of the BTC) was spending half his day grappling with the shadow organisation. He sent for me to assist him and I soon shared my chief's incredulity at the curiously amateurish way in which the Commission was being set up, in an attic of the London Transport general offices at 55 Broadway.

The LNER officers resolved to place on record their loyalty to the Board, which they did by having printed a presentation volume handed to each of the Directors, recalling the achievements of the LNER with pride. It constituted, in the words of the preface, 'a token of appreciation of the kindness which they have always received from the Directors and of gratitude for the cordial friendship between the Board and the Management which throughout the lifetime of the Company the Directors have done so much to promote.' The volume was signed by 66 senior officers, among whom I was proud to be included.

At midnight on 31 December 1947 the LNER was vested in the British Transport Commission, as posters exhibited at stations informed the travelling public, most of whom had not the faintest idea what sort of animal such a Commission might be. The Company, however, as distinct from the railway, had to continue in existence for a few months yet, to tidy up various odds and ends and to declare a final dividend for 1947.

At the last Annual General Meeting the

Chairman of the LNER Stockholders Association paid a graceful tribute to Sir Ronald Matthews and the Board for the work they had done to protect, as far as possible, the interests of the stockholders. A motion was also proposed to allot a sum of £63,000 to be divided among the Directors as compensation for loss of office. But on a show of hands, the motion was lost. The shareholders were scarcely more grateful than the Government had shown itself to be!

The chief way in which the LNER can be said to have survived since its absorption into BR is in the number of top managers it has provided over many years for the nationalised system. Of course, by now most of today's senior executives probably joined the service after 1947; but even so, if their early training was on those parts of BR that were formerly LNER, they probably sensed and benefited from the traditions that linger at York and other places in the railway heartland, best described as a sense of historic continuity linked with a highly progressive outlook. Traditions established by Whitelaw, Wedgwood and Robert Bell have survived nationalisation, largely because they can be summed up in the LNER motto, 'Forward'.

Appendix 1: LNER Chairmen and principal Chief Officers

Chairman
William Whitelaw	1923–38
Sir Ronald W. Matthews	1938–48

Deputy Chairman
Lord Faringdon	1923–34
Sir Murrough J. Wilson	1934–46
W. K. Whigham	1946–48

Joint Secretaries to the Company
James McLaren }	
G. F. Thurston }	1923–25

Secretary to the Company
James McLaren	1925–38
P. J. Dowsett	1938–42
W. H. Johnson	1943–48

Chief General Manager
Sir Ralph L. Wedgwood	1923–39
Sir Charles H. Newton	1939–47
Miles Beevor (acting)	1947

Divisional General Manager (Southern Area)
S. A. Parnwell	1923–24
Alexander Wilson	1924–29
G. F. Thurston	1929–36
C. H. Newton	1937–39
H. H. Mauldin	1939–41
George Mills	1941–45
V. M. Barrington-Ward	1945–47

Divisional General Manager (North Eastern Area)
Alexander Wilson	1923–24
George Davidson	1924–28
Thomas Hornsby	1928–36
C. M. Jenkin Jones	1936–47

General Manager (Scotland)
James Calder	1923–34

Divisional General Manager (Scottish Area)
George Mills	1934–41
R. J. M. Inglis	1941–44
T. F. Cameron	1944–47

Chief Legal Adviser
Sir Francis Dunnell	1923–28
I. Buchanan Pritchard	1928–43
Miles Beevor	1943–47

Chief Accountant
C. L. Edwards	1923–28
C. H. Newton	1928–36
G. Sutherland	1936–42
L. C. Glenister	1942–47

Chief Mechanical Engineer
Sir Nigel Gresley	1923–41
Edward Thompson	1941–46
A. H. Peppercorn	1946–47

Chief Engineer
J. C. L. Train	1942–47

Note: Titles are shown as at conclusion of term of office.

Appendix 2:
The LNER East Coast Diesel Scheme of 1947

24th July, 1947

MEMORANDUM TO THE JOINT LOCOMOTIVE AND TRAFFIC COMMITTEES

DIESEL-ELECTRIC TRACTION ON THE L.N.E.R.

INTRODUCTION

1 The L.N.E.R. traffic difficulties of the present day are largely due to the non-availability of Steam Locomotive power, which in turn is substantially affected by the following factors:

(a) Inability to obtain delivery of new locomotives either from contractors or railway shops as rapidly as had been hoped;
(b) Excessive amount of repairs required due to high average age of existing locomotives;
(c) Shortage of coal;
(d) Inferior quality of coal.

2 Other considerations affect the availability of steam locomotive power but the four mentioned above are sufficiently important to warrant examination of the possibility of developing some other form of traction, thus opening out an additional source of new building and easing the demand for good quality coal of which supplies presumably will continue to be short for a considerable period. The alternatives considered are as follows:

(a) *Main Line Electrification* – This can only proceed gradually and at very great first cost in materials and time, and, to be justified, it must include all railway traffic passing over the section of line concerned. Conversion must be carried out section by section, and for this reason it would be some years before electrification could cover the whole of the main line between London and Edinburgh.

(b) *Gas-Turbo-Electric Locomotives* – If it is proved possible to build a Gas-Turbo-Electric Locomotive of say 3,000 brake horse power delivered to the generator within the British loading gauge, so that the equipment can be contained on one locomotive underframe, such a locomotive would be suitable for the heavy trains on the Anglo-Scottish services. In view, however, of the development work that still requires to be carried out in connection with Gas-Turbo-Electric Locomotives, some time must elapse before sufficient practical experience will be available.

(c) *Diesel-Electric Locomotives* – Many of the advantages of electric traction, such as higher availability, better operating conditions and simpler maintenance methods, can be achieved with a less initial capital expenditure but with greater flexibility by the use of Diesel-electric locomotives and it is suggested that the latter provides a more attractive proposition for the immediate future without prejudicing the eventual adoption of main line electrification if and when this can be justified by traffic conditions.

3 As regards the coal shortage, the Government have decided that the railways should reduce their demands for coal by burning oil fuel and the appropriate and very costly conversion work is in hand, but only about 1½ tons of coal will be saved for every ton of fuel oil burnt in a locomotive firebox, which is a short-term and most uneconomic method of effecting a saving in coal. On the other hand, in the case of modern Diesel-electric locomotives about 5 tons of coal would be saved for every ton of diesel fuel oil required.

L.N.E.R. EXPERIENCE WITH
DIESEL-ELECTRIC SHUNTING ENGINES

4 The L.N.E.R. have already at work at Whitemoor four Diesel-electric shunting engines which have fully proved themselves in hump and flat shunting work.

5 Experience with them has been so satisfactory as to justify acquiring further units for marshalling work. The complete "Dieselization" of Whitemoor is being examined, and schemes for other places in all three Areas are being worked out.

6 A condition that must be faced is that special provision will have to be made for the maintenance of the Diesel-electric engines that cannot, because of their specialized maintenance technique, be satisfactorily accommodated alongside steam locomotives in ordinary locomotive running sheds. It is true that at Whitemoor improvised arrangements have been made but they must be replaced by permanent and separate accommodation, and it is realized by all concerned that specially skilled and trained staff for maintaining both the Diesel engines and the electric traction equipment on a definite routine basis are required.

7 The possibility of embarking on a more ambitious scheme of Diesel-electric development has therefore been examined.

U.S.A. DEVELOPMENT OF MAIN LINE
DIESEL-ELECTRIC LOCOMOTIVES

8 As the Directors will recollect from the reports of the Chief Mechanical Engineer and the Chief Electrical Engineer on their visit to America, and from articles in the Press, the trend in Diesel-electric traction in the U.S.A. has for some years been towards the use of independent motive power units for both passenger and freight service. U.S.A. practice is now based largely on 2,000 h.p. units for express passenger work, 1,500 h.p. units for mixed traffic or freight and 1,000 h.p. units for shunting work or transfer trip work. For main-line working, passenger and freight, the units can be combined under multiple-unit control into (for passenger service) 4,000 h.p. or (for freight service) 6,000 h.p. "locomotives", operated by one driver and an assistant driver.

9 The introduction of Diesel-electric tractive units in this form means that the changeover from steam traction involves merely the replacement of one form of independent locomotive by another, the train vehicles, whether passenger or freight, being those that would be used behind a steam locomotive. No question thus arises (as it did in the early days of Diesel-electric) of designing special or lightweight passenger stock. The problem is thus simplified considerably and direct comparisons between the two forms of traction can be more easily made.

10 The efficiency and reliability of Diesel-electric power units for long distance trains are already proved – so far as American practice is concerned – so that it would appear that a large scale trial of the units under British conditions can reasonably be contemplated in preference to the limited experiments which alone would be appropriate if motive power of completely unknown capabilities were in question. The smaller loading gauge of this country compared with the U.S.A. may introduce certain difficulties in design, and this question is referred to again later in this memorandum.

APPLICATION TO L.N.E.R. EAST COAST SERVICES

11　It is suggested that the development of a sound scheme for the use of Diesel-electric units on the L.N.E.R. can be achieved only by taking as a full-scale example a particular and important group of our passenger services.

12　An essential feature of Diesel-electric locomotives is their capacity for continuous operation without refuelling or other attention over much longer distances than steam locomotives, and it is on the East Coast passenger services that the fullest trial of the additional availability of the Diesel-electric units could be made.

13　The trailing load of these services may be taken as 520 tons, and it is considered that in order to deal adequately with the trains, and possibly introduce a limited degree of acceleration, two Diesel-electric locomotive units of 1,600 brake horse power at the generator coupling, making a total locomotive power of 3,200 brake horse power, equivalent to approximately 2,400 rail h.p. at the driving wheels, and operated by multiple-unit control, would be required. Comparative particulars of a "Pacific" steam locomotive and a 'double-unit' Diesel-electric locomotive are:

	Steam Traction	Diesel-electric Traction	
	"Pacific" Locomotive	*Locomotive Unit*	*Double-Unit Locomotive*
Wheel Formation	4-6-2	6-6	6-6-6-6
Max. Permissible Speed – M.P.H.	100	100	100
Total Weight in Working Order – Tons	161	120	240
Number of Driving Axles	3	4	8
Total Adhesive Weight – Tons	66	80	160
Starting Tractive Effort at 25% Adhesion – lb.	37,000	40,350	80,700
Tractive Effort at 60 M.P.H. – lb.	11,900	6,725	13,450
Tractive Effort at 75 M.P.H. – lb.	11,000	6,450	12,900
Length over Buffers	73' 2"	57' 0"	114' 0"
Rigid/Truck Wheel Base	14' 6"	15' 0"	15' 0"
Diesel Engines	–	One 1,600 H.P.	Two 1,600 H.P.
Diesel Engine Speed – R.P.M.	–	750	750

Note: The Diesel-electric tractive effort given does not include amount required for 79 tons additional locomotive weight which is, of course, provided.

14　A scheme has therefore been developed providing for the operation by Diesel-electric traction of the principal trains in each direction between London and Edinburgh, involving a total passenger train mileage of approximately 2,460,000 annually.

15　The services concerned are detailed in Appendix A and would require ten double-unit locomotives in traffic. To provide this number and in addition to cover for each unit:

(i)　Servicing and maintenance routine at the Main Depot for about 6 to 8 hours in each 48 hours;

(ii)　Periodical overhaul in the Main Depot for two weeks every year;

(iii)　General overhaul at Main Depot or C.M.E.'s works, for three weeks every three years,

a total stock of 22 single units would be needed. In order, however, to cover service repairs that might take longer than the normal maintenance between daily diagrammed workings an additional single unit should be provided and it would be prudent to guard against the effects of derailment or traffic diversions by the provision of a further complete double-unit locomotive.

16　The total stock of Diesel-electric single units should therefore be 25 with an average train mileage per double-unit locomotive of about 196,800 annually. By their provision it would be possible to save 26 "Pacific" engines in traffic or (allowing for the availability of steam locomotives) 32 engines in the stock.

MAINTENANCE

17 From the descriptions of American practice that have appeared in reports and technical journals it is obvious that the maintenance of Diesel-electric locomotives requires to be specially planned both as regards the accommodation and the staff.

18 As has already been pointed out, separate and specialized maintenance accommodation is an essential, and the fact that this must be provided whatever the number of main line Diesel-electric locomotives introduced supports the idea of a large scale experiment against that of introducing, for example, one locomotive for trial; in the latter case the experiment would be so completely overloaded with overhead charges as to be unrealistic.

19 The servicing and running maintenance of the Diesel-electric locomotives working in the Anglo-Scottish services could best be arranged with a main maintenance depot at or near one terminus with a subsidiary maintenance depot at or near the other.

20 Considerable difficulty would be experienced in finding a site for a main depot in the neighbourhood of King's Cross but a suitable site can be found near Edinburgh where the release of locomotives from incoming trains is much easier than from "dead-end" platforms at King's Cross, and where, moreover, it is thought that skilled staff could be obtained more readily than in London. The site proposed is part of Leith Central Station, two miles from Waverley and giving accommodation for housing 4 or 5 double-unit locomotives. The proposed facilities are described in more detail in Appendix 'B' and are estimated to cost £200,000.

21 The subsidiary depot should be as near King's Cross as possible and consideration is being given to possible sites at either Finsbury Park Goods Yard or Holloway Cattle Sidings. The facilities proposed are also described in Appendix 'B' and it is estimated that the cost will be about £60,000.

22 If the inspection and maintenance can be carried out on the same systematic mileage basis as in the U.S.A., the total facilities proposed are thought to be adequate to deal with not less than twice the number of locomotive units contemplated for the initial scheme, but it has been thought wise to allow a generous margin in planning them.

FUEL COSTS

23 To make a direct comparison between steam and Diesel-electric fuel costs on a British main line is difficult owing to the absence of practical experience with the newer design. As a preliminary, however, certain general estimates can be put forward showing the ratio of fuel costs as between steam and Diesel-electric locomotives.

24 These general estimates are as follows:

(i) *Overall Thermo-Dynamic Efficiency from Fuel to Rail*

Steam	6%
Diesel-Electric	24%

(ii) *Fuel Costs per Ton*

Coal	£2
Diesel Engine Oil	£8

(iii) *Fuel Consumption for trailing load of 520 tons from King's Cross to Edinburgh – 393 miles*

	Tons
Steam @ 60 lb. of coal per train mile	10.52
Diesel-Electric @ 12 lb. of fuel oil per train mile	2.10

(iv) *Fuel Costs per Train Mile for King's Cross to Edinburgh Service*

	d.
Steam	12.84
Diesel-Electric	10.28

CONSTRUCTION COSTS

25 The ascertainment of the probable construction costs of Diesel-electric engines for L.N.E.R. main line service is not easy. Only the average costs of American output are quotable, and it was understood that at the end of 1945 these were, in English money:

Main Line	
2,000 h.p. Diesel-Electric loco. unit	£45,000
1,500 h.p. Diesel-Electric loco. unit	£31,250
Shunting	
1,000 h.p. Diesel-Electric loco. unit	£20,000

At that time it was also stated in America that the cost of a Diesel-electric locomotive was approximately double the cost of a Steam locomotive of the same power.

26 In America, certain manufacturers have been turning out a limited number of types of more or less standard Diesel-electric locomotives in very large numbers with in effect mass production methods, and this has naturally helped to bring the cost down. In addition, the larger loading gauge in America has facilitated the use of Diesel engines of relatively large power on one underframe.

27 In this country, with its smaller loading gauge, only one manufacturer (the English Electric Company) has so far undertaken the provision of a 1,600 h.p. engine in a single unit, so that two locomotive units will comprise a 3,200 h.p. locomotive. It has recently been announced that the L.M.S. have ordered two Diesel-electric "double-unit" locomotives of this capacity from the English Electric Company.

28 The estimated cost of the 32 "Pacific" Steam locomotives that would be displaced and deleted from Building Programmes, would be £16,000 per locomotive (Company's workshops costs) making a total cost of £512,000.

It is estimated that the cost at present-day prices of the 25 Diesel-electric locomotives units required would be as follows:

	Per Loco. Unit £	Total £
Diesel Engines and Electric Traction Equipment	36,000	900,000
Mechanical parts, if built at Doncaster @ £130 per ton	9,100	227,500
	£45,100	£1,127,500

TOTAL FIRST COSTS

29 To the cost of 25 such Diesel-electric locomotive units, £1,127,500, there must be added about £260,000 for the necessary maintenance and repair facilities at Edinburgh and King's Cross, making approximately £1,390,000 in all or about £880,000 more than the cost of the "Pacific" locomotives displaced.

The purchase of units from the U.S.A. may be contemplated, but questions regarding foreign exchange will arise. Besides, the loading gauge difference as mentioned above is so considerable as between Britain and the U.S.A. that standard U.S.A. models would need considerable redesigning to suit L.N.E.R. requirements.

STAFF

The question of staff is important. Maintenance staff would have to be recruited partly from the employees of the manufacturers, and partly from specially trained and intelligent men selected from the Railway Company's existing staff, but the training of steam drivers to operate Diesel-electric locomotives should present no special difficulty.

OPERATING COSTS

31 The estimated total Operating Costs comprising:

Depreciation
General overhaul and Repairs
Inspection and Running Maintenance
Train Working Costs – including Enginemen's
  Wages and Fuel

with an annual train mileage of 2,460,000 are detailed in Appendix 'C' hereto [not reprinted] and are summarized as follows:

	Steam £	Diesel-electric £
Depreciation	9,600	46,200
General Overhaul and Repairs	64,000	43,800
Inspection and Running Maintenance	38,400	25,000
Train Working Costs:		
Drivers and Firemen	65,800	67,800
Fuel	131,600	105,400
Fuel handling etc.	5,000	2,000
Total	£314,400	£290,200
Per Train Mile	30.7d.	28.3d.

In accordance with the above estimates there would be an annual saving in Train Operating Costs of £24,200 which is equivalent to about 2.75% on the additional outlay of about £880,000.

SUMMARY OF CONCLUSIONS

32 This outline of a scheme for the possible introduction of main line Diesel-electric traction on the L.N.E.R. may be summarized as follows:

(i) Main line Diesel-electric traction has proved its efficiency in other countries.

(ii) Its most modern developments have taken the shape of independent locomotive units hauling trains of ordinary vehicles.

(iii) Special maintenance accommodation and staff are essential for the efficient operation of Diesel-electric locomotives whatever the scope of any trials carried out.

(iv) Therefore, to be realistically economic, an experiment with main line Diesel-electric development should have a reasonably wide basis.

(v) Our East Coast Anglo-Scottish services offer the best field for the employment of the Diesels' high availability and capacity for long-distance running.

(vi) The initial outlay for 25 Diesel-electric locomotive units is estimated at £1,127,500 and about £260,000 for maintenance establishments – a total of about £1,390,000. The comparable outlay for the equivalent steam power – estimated at 32 "Pacifics" – would be £512,000 at L.N.E.R. Workshop prices.

(vii) The operating costs would appear to be in the ratio of:

Diesel-electric	92.2
Steam	100.0

It is understood that in the U.S.A. the costs per train mile of Diesel-electric locomotive operation are about two-thirds those of steam operation. The difference as compared with the estimates for British conditions arises because –

(a) the first cost of our buying a Diesel-electric "double-unit" locomotive in this country is expected (para. 28 above) under present conditions to be 5½ times that of our building a replaced steam locomotive of lesser power; in the U.S.A. the ratio is 2 to 1 in the case of locomotives of approximately similar power;

(b) the cost of Diesel oil in Britain is expected to be about three times that applying in the U.S.A.;

(c) the annual mileage run per engine by Diesel-electric locomotives in the U.S.A. is understood to be greater than is contemplated for the L.N.E.R. Anglo-Scottish services.

(viii) Annual savings are probably equivalent to nearly 3.0% on the additional first cost of Diesel-electric units and their maintenance establishments compared with the steam locomotives.

(ix) Apart from the direct financial case the following advantages may safely be claimed for Diesel-electric traction:

(a) Increased availability

(b) Higher acceleration and better performance on adverse gradients.

(c) Cleanliness.

(d) Publicity and prestige value.

(x) The building of Diesel-electrics by outside Contractors who would not be interested in the construction of steam locomotives opens up an alternative source of supply of express passenger motive power and frees capacity for the building of additional mixed traffic or freight steam engines.

(xi) The alternative possibilities of adopting Gas-Turbine propulsion or Main Line Electrification are considered to be less attractive under present circumstances than a large-scale trial of Diesel-electric main line traction, particularly as the adoption of this method would not preclude its replacement in due course by either of the alternatives if these should prove to be more economical.

RECOMMENDATIONS

33 It is therefore RECOMMENDED:

(i) that the experiment on the lines set out with 25

Diesel-electric locomotive units in replacement of 32 "Pacific" steam locomotives should be approved in principle; and

(ii) that enquiries be made of all possible builders of Diesel-electric locomotives and designs and quotations obtained.

APPROVED by the Board.

APPENDIX 'A' –
DIESEL-ELECTRIC TRACTION
ON THE L.N.E.R.

Trains to be covered by means of 25 locomotive units

	Weekdays	*Sundays*
Edinburgh to	10.00 am	
King's Cross	10.15 am	11.15 am
	1.10 pm	11.25 am
	7.50 pm	7.50 pm
	9.30 pm (SX)	9.30 pm
	10.00 pm	10.00 pm
	10.20 pm	10.20 pm
	10.40 pm	10.40 pm
King's Cross to	1.00 am	
Edinburgh	9.45 am	
	10.00 am	11.00 am
	1.00 pm	11.20 am

7.05 pm (SX)	7.05 pm
7.30 pm	7.30 pm
8.20 pm (SO)	
10.15 pm	10.15 pm
10.30 pm	10.30 pm

In addition, the following trains have been included in order to provide for the full employment of the Diesel-electric locomotive units in traffic:

	Weekdays	*Sundays*
Aberdeen to		
Edinburgh	9.10 am	–
Doncaster to		
King's Cross	1.32 pm	–
Grantham to		
King's Cross	1.21 pm	12.58 pm
Edinburgh to		
Aberdeen	3.40 am	–
King's Cross to		
Doncaster	8.55 am	–
King's Cross to		
Grantham	9.15 am	10.00 am

Total train mileage: 2,460,000 (approx) per annum

C.G.M.O.
July 1947

Index